Bridge
The Acol System of Bidding

TERENCE REESE is a world champion
and the author of some fifty books
on bridge, poker, canasta, backgammon
and casino games. Always an exponent
of the flexible and aggressive Acol
system, he shows the reader how to
use his brains and not rely on 'point
count' or any set rules or priorities.
'Relying on judgement,' he observes
tersely, 'at least you will learn from
your mistakes.'

ALBERT DORMER, a chartered surveyor
by profession, has gained a worldwide
reputation as editor of *World Bridge
News* and of the *Bulletin of the
International Bridge Press Association*.
He has collaborated with Terence
Reese in many books, including *How to
Play a Good Game of Bridge* (published
in Pan Books), *The Complete Book
of Bridge*, and *The Play of the Cards*.

Bridge
The Acol System of Bidding
A MODERN VERSION OF THE ACOL SYSTEM TODAY

Terence Reese · Albert Dormer

Pan Books · London and Sydney

Originally published 1961 by Edward Arnold (Publishers) Ltd
as *The Acol System Today*
This fully revised edition published 1978 by Pan Books Ltd,
Cavaye Place, London SW10 9PG
2nd printing 1980
© Terence Reese and Albert Dormer 1961, 1978
ISBN 0 330 25540 1
Printed and bound in Great Britain by
Richard Clay (The Chaucer Press) Ltd, Bungay, Suffolk

Foreword

This book bears a cousinly relationship to *The Acol System Today*, which was first published in 1961. Where a point was expressed in that book as well as we could express it now, we have let the original copy stand. We have dispensed with the quizzes, which gave the text the appearance of an examination test.

The system has shown immense vitality and flexibility over the years, adopting many new concepts without losing its essential character. Theorists who like to have everything tied and labelled say that Acol is unscientific. 'Non-scientific' would be a better word.

Parts I and II describe what in the text we call the factory model. Part III contains the optional extras found in the racing model. It is interesting to observe that there has been a 75% change in these since the last account. The newcomers – notably, the transfer responses over 1NT, competitive doubles, unassuming cue-bids, negative doubles – are far more substantial and are certain to last.

TERENCE REESE
ALBERT DORMER

Contents

PART 1 THE UNCONTESTED AUCTION

The standard opening

In Acol the majority of hands in the 13 to 20 point range, unless suitable for 1NT or a strong Two bid, are opened with One of a suit. But minimum hands that lack playing strength should be passed.

♠ Q J   ♡ 8 6 5 3   ◇ K Q J   ♣ A 7 4 2

If partner cannot speak, this hand will be better in the middle. There is no suit that cries out to be bid and the fact that the hand is weak in defence to a spade contract makes it unwise to initiate the contest.

Hands containing a strong suit, however, may well justify a light tactical opening.

The tactical opening

To open the bidding is a good move in itself. It is like batting first on a good wicket. You hope to score well yourself, but if it turns out that the opponents are stronger then at any rate you make the pitch less good for them.

That is why Acol players are willing to open on 'shape': that is to say, on hands that contain no more than a fair share of high cards but are likely to take more than a fair share of tricks. The following are examples:

♠ A Q 10 9 7 2   ♡ 9 5   ◇ A 10 3   ♣ 8 3

A man can miss a game by passing that hand. Make the Ace of Diamonds the King and it is still good tactics to open One Spade.

♠ 10 8 4 3   ♡ K J 9 7 4   ◇ 3   ♣ A K 5

Here you are on less firm ground in opening One Heart, for the suit is not strong and the hand will develop few tricks if you find no fit in your partner's hand. Against that, the fact that you have values in the major suits justifies an opening bid.

♠ Q 10 6 ♥ 8 ♦ 9 8 2 ♣ A K J 10 5 3

It is not likely that a One Club opening will take the bread out of the opponents' mouths, but it is a forward move and the good suit is your protection against over-reaching. Third or fourth in hand, Three Clubs would be the sensible bid.

In opening borderline hands a player needs to keep a sharp edge on his judgement. Here are some of the considerations that should be taken into account:

The texture of the hand

By 'texture' is meant the disposition of the high cards in relation to the long suits. The attacking power of a hand is enhanced if the strength lies with the length.

(1) ♠ 4 2 ♥ A Q 8 7 2 ♦ A Q 9 3 ♣ 8 5

(2) ♠ A 4 ♥ J 8 7 4 2 ♦ Q 9 6 3 ♣ A Q

The first hand is a sound opening because the high cards will help to establish the long cards. The second is a weak opening because the high cards are mainly outside the long suits.

The major suit holdings

It seldom pays to force the pace when you are weak in the majors. You may jockey the enemy into a good contract which they would otherwise have missed.

A small doubleton or trebleton in a major suit that may be called against you is an unfavourable holding. It means that trumps will break well for the opposition. If you have a void or a singleton, on the other hand, there is a chance that partner will have length in their suit and you need have fewer qualms about opening a minimum hand.

Vulnerability

This may influence the decision on borderline hands when the main suit is broken. For example:

♠ 8 ♥ Q 10 8 5 3 ♦ A J 7 6 ♣ A 10 2

Not vulnerable, this is a possible One Heart opening. If the hands fit you should make a contract or achieve a profitable sacrifice, while on the misfitting hands you will often go down in fifties.

Vulnerable, however, it would be a poor opening, for you can seldom sacrifice at that score and if you run into a misfit a double will be more expensive.

Third-hand openings

One of the aims of the light third-hand opening is to promote a good defence. A borderline hand should not be opened if a lead of the bid suit would not be welcome.

(1) ♠ 9 2   ♡ Q 9 7 6 4   ◇ K Q 6   ♣ A 10 3

(2) ♠ 8 5   ♡ A Q J 4 2   ◇ 7 4 3   ♣ K 9 5

The first hand should not be opened in any position but the second is a fair third-hand opening since it gives partner a good lead.

Another aspect of third-hand tactics is the possibility of deflecting the enemy from their best contract. The policy here is to wait for a genuine opportunity rather than to make random bluff bids.

♠ J 9 8 5   ♡ 10 9 6 2   ◇ A K Q   ♣ 9 4

You have a good defence to a major suit contract, so you judge that the opponents' game, if they have one, is in notrumps. Try opening One Diamond: the chances are that they have no diamond guard and will fight shy of notrumps, not knowing that yours is a short suit.

The choice of suit

As in all systems, a player who opens the bidding must be prepared to bid again over a suit response (unless his partner has passed originally). It is necessary to state at this point the qualifications for certain rebids, because these affect the choice of opening.

The standard for an opening 1NT is 12–14 not vulnerable, 15–17 vulnerable. The standard for a *rebid* of 1NT is the opposite. That is to say, a player who rebids 1NT when not vulnerable is assumed to hold 15–16 (not 17), and a player who rebids 1NT when vulnerable is assumed to hold the equivalent of a weak notrump opening, 12–14. This is sometimes called the 'converse principle'. It is an advance in bidding theory since the last account of the Acol system.

The standard for a rebid of 2NT, when partner has responded at the Two level, is 15–17. Thus a player who opens on a minimum 13 or so must consider carefully whether he will have a sound rebid over any response at the Two level.

4–3–3–3

When a balanced hand does not fall into the appropriate range for 1 NT, it may be necessary to open with a prepared bid of One Club.

♠ K 10 3   ♡ A Q 8 5   ◇ J 6 2   ♣ K 10 7

Vulnerable, it would be unsound to open One Heart because you would have no good rebid over a response of Two Diamonds or Two Clubs. The only practical opening is One Club.

♠ K 10 3   ♡ A Q 8 5   ◇ Q J 2   ♣ K 10 7

Now you have 15 points, plus two 10s. Vulnerable, you would open 1NT. Not vulnerable, you could theoretically open One Heart, intending to rebid 2NT; but One Club would be a better choice, for remember that, in accordance with the converse principle, a rebid of 1NT would express your values accurately.

4–4–3–2

When the hand falls into the appropriate range, usually open 1NT. Otherwise:

Open the higher of touching suits but with clubs and spades open One Club.

With non-touching suits, spades and diamonds or hearts and clubs, it is generally right to open the lower-ranking suit.

♠ K J 5 4   ♡ 10 8   ◇ K 10 8 3   ♣ A Q 4

One Diamond is the best (vulnerable) opening. If you open One Spade and partner bids Two Hearts you have no sound rebid since you lack the strength for 2NT or Three Diamonds and your spades are not rebiddable.

On a certain type of hand One Spade may be preferable to One Diamond.

♠ A J 6 3   ♡ 10 7 2   ◇ A K 9 3   ♣ J 2

The objection to One Diamond here is that you will have no sound rebid over Two Clubs. You can, however, open One Spade, intending to bid Two Diamonds over Two Clubs, and to raise Two Hearts to Three Hearts. As we shall see later, a response of Two Hearts normally implies a five-card suit.

4-4-4-1

When each of the three suits is worth bidding, the general rule is to open the suit below the singleton. That caters for any response from partner.

♠ Q J 9 2   ♡ 6   ◇ A K 7 6   ♣ K Q 7 3

Open One Diamond. If partner bids hearts you can show the spades, while if he bids clubs you have strong support.

When one of the suits is weak it is better to treat the hand as a two-suiter rather than a three-suiter. Choose between these two suits according to texture and the necessity of having a sound rebid.

♠ 9   ♡ J 8 5 3   ◇ A K J 7   ♣ A J 10 7

The hearts do not demand expression, so you treat this as a diamond–club hand and open One Diamond.

♠ A J 7 3   ♡ 7   ◇ Q 8 5 3   ♣ A K 10 5

Here the diamonds are weak and One Club is the best opening.

With 4-4-1-4 One Heart is often preferred to One Club when the opener is better than minimum and can rebid 2NT over Two Diamonds.

5-4-3-1 or 5-4-2-2

The five-card suit is generally opened but there are certain hands of minimum honour strength that call for different treatment. Firstly, minimum hands where the suits are touching and the five-card suit is lower ranking:

♠ K 6   ♡ K Q 10 6   ◇ A J 8 4 2   ♣ 9 5

If you open One Diamond you may never get a chance to bid hearts. A reverse bid of Two Hearts over, say, a One Spade response would suggest a stronger hand. Since the heart holding is good it is better to open One Heart and rebid Two Diamonds.

On the next hand the five-card suit is the one to open.

♠ K 8 5 4   ♡ A Q J 9 2   ◊ Q 10   ♣ 8 6

Apart from the fact that the spades are weak, the hearts are rebiddable. Spades can be left on the shelf until such time as partner introduces them.

5–5

Generally bid the higher-ranking suit first except where the suits are clubs and spades. The reason for opening the higher-ranking suit is that it leaves you better placed on the next round.

♠ K J 8 5 3   ♡ 7   ◊ A 10 6 4 2   ♣ A 3

Having opened One Spade you will probably be able to show diamonds later. True, if partner's response is Two Hearts your correct bid will be Two Spades, for you are not strong enough for Three Diamonds. But your spades are rebiddable and it is less serious to conceal a minor suit than a fairly strong major.

If you open One Diamond and partner responds 1NT or Two Clubs you cannot introduce the spades without overstating your general strength, and even if you do mention spades on the second round partner will not necessarily read you for a five-timer.

With five clubs and five spades, an opening One Club leaves more space for development. With a moderate hand containing a fair spade suit, however, One Spade is a better defensive measure, as it is more difficult to overcall.

When one suit is strong and the other weak it is better to open the strong suit except when the suits are adjacent.

♠ A 7   ♡ 10 8 7 6 3   ◊ 5   ♣ A K J 4 2

Open One Club and, if partner bids One Spade, rebid Two Clubs. That is a lesser evil than opening One Heart and perhaps having to rebid that anaemic holding. Had the suits been touching, however, say hearts and diamonds, it would have been right to open the higher suit irrespective of top cards.

The above observations are a general guide for the majority of occasions, but the authors have not set out to compile a drill book that must be followed without reference to tactical considerations. Heel-clicking attitudes have no place in Acol.

Here are some examples where judgement will produce a different answer from theory.

♠ 10 9 6 2   ♡ Q 8 5 4   ◇ A 9   ♣ A K 4

One Club is preferable to One Heart or One Spade. Avoid the introduction of weak major suits if there is a reasonable alternative. Acol players do not share the view of those scientific writers who equate A K Q 10 with 5 4 3 2.

♠ K J 7 3   ♡ A J 8 3   ◇ Q 10 5   ♣ A 10

For a number of reasons the best (non-vulnerable) opening is One Heart, not One Spade. You can bid 2NT over Two Clubs or Two Diamonds and if partner does not mention spades you will not miss anything there.

♠ A Q   ♡ K J 9 4   ◇ A 6 2   ♣ Q 10 8 3

Not vulnerable, open One Diamond and bid 2NT over a response of One Spade or Two Clubs. Once in a while it will turn out badly, partner valuing his hand wrongly because of your diamond bid. Much more often you will play the hand in notrumps and the semi-psychic One Diamond will work to your advantage.

We treat this subject in a new way, starting from the proposition that responding hands belong to one of three categories – weak, medium or strong. Thus we shall examine:

1. *Weak hands* of about 6 to 9 points. These are generally worth only one forward move, so one looks for a way to express the main features of the hand in a single bid.

2. *Medium hands* in the 10 to 12 point range where the prospects of game will depend upon the strength shown by the opener's rebid. Here the player must look ahead: he selects his first response with the thought in mind that he may well follow up with a further effort on the second round.

3. *Strong hands*, usually of opening strength, on which the responder will not stop short of game. Since on these hands he does not fear competition there is a better case for leisurely investigation. The first response need not express the full character of the hand.

You may find a parallel in the manoeuvres of the fashion trade, where the vendors of inexpensive goods place them in the forefront of their window display; those of a superior class have a thought for lighting and montage; while in *haute couture* the approach is sometimes indirect, by way of an elegant accessory.

1. Weak hands

Here the choice is between a raise of partner's suit, a response of 1NT, or a minimum bid in a new suit.

Single raise of partner's suit

This raise is based on supporting tricks which may be in high cards or purely distributional. When you raise One Heart to Two Hearts partner will take you to have at least:

(1) ♠ 8 4	♡ Q 10 7 2	◇ 9 8 4	♣ A 7 5 2
(2) ♠ 9 6 5 3	♡ J 10 6 4 3	◇ Q 7 4	♣ 8

Note that we said that *partner* would regard these as minimum bids, not that they *were* the minimum on which a raise should be given.

♠ K 7 6 3   ♡ 10 4   ◇ J 8 6 2   ♣ 9 7 4

It is generally advisable on tactical grounds to raise One Spade to Two Spades, though of course the hand is under strength and you are quite likely to go down in whatever contract is reached. It is the same as with sub-minimum opening bids: you risk misleading partner because good bidding has to be competitive as well as constructive.

At the other end are hands that are top weight for a single raise but present no good alternative.

♠ K Q J 3   ♡ A 9 4   ◇ 7 5 4   ♣ 10 8 2

A simple Two Spades is better than either Three Spades or a waiting bid in a short suit. On the whole it is wise to keep something in hand during the early rounds of a constructive (as opposed to competitive) auction rather than to run out of breath at the first stage.

When the choice is between raising partner and bidding a new suit there is a well-established principle in favour of supporting partner, especially when his suit is a major.

♠ J 8 4 2   ♡ K 10 4   ◇ 9 3   ♣ K 7 6 3

Raise One Heart to Two. It is the most valuable information you can convey in one bid.

That principle applies with extra force when the responder has previously passed.

♠ J 9 8   ♡ K J 6 2   ◇ 5 4   ♣ A 9 7 4

Partner opens One Spade. Not having passed, you are just good enough for a temporizing bid of Two Clubs. Having passed, you must raise the spades and not risk being left in Two Clubs.

1NT response

This is the standard response on balanced hands of about 6 to 9 points that present neither a sound raise nor a suit that can sensibly be bid at the range of One. In such a well-trodden field we can most usefully look at a few hands that create a small problem.

♠ K 7 3   ♡ 7 5 4   ◇ J 9 3 2   ♣ A 8 6

Clearly ideal for 1NT over One Heart, and because of the balanced distribution 1NT is also the best response to any other opening.

♠ 8 7 5 4   ♡ K J   ◇ A Q 6   ♣ 9 5 3 2

Ten points or no, there is no sensible alternative to 1NT in response to One Heart. We would favour the same bid in response to One Diamond or One Club.

♠ 7   ♡ 9 4   ◇ K 10 7 5 4 3   ♣ Q 8 6 5

An awkward type of hand for the system. It is dangerous to respond 1NT to One Spade with a minimum in high cards and a singleton in partner's suit. And if the opening bid is One Heart, a response of 1NT is inapt because of the singleton spade. Nor, as we shall see later, can Two Diamonds be considered.

Although a game can be missed if partner happens to fit the diamonds, we recommend a pass. Pin your hopes to the chance that the opponents may reopen.

♠ 9 7   ♡ 7 3 2   ◇ J 9 5 4 2   ♣ A K 8

Here you respond 1NT to One Spade and over One Heart have to choose between 1NT with a poor holding in spades and Two Hearts with inadequate trump support. Our preference is for Two Hearts as the 8 points include a crisp A K.

♠ J 7 6   ♡ K 10 2   ◇ Q 9 6 3   ♣ 5 4 2

Over One Heart or One Spade the bid is 1NT, but over One Club you should respond One Diamond. There is a general understanding that 1NT in response to One Club shows better than a minimum – say 8 to 10 points.

Response in a new suit

Partner will expect 6 points or more from a response at the One level, but the bid can be made with less on a good suit: K Q x x̄ x, for example, or K 10 x x x x and a Jack outside.

There is no definite upper limit but as will be seen later a force is in order on most 16-point hands.

With two suits of unequal length which can be bid at the range of One, the usual rule is to bid the longer.

♠ A Q 7 3　　♡ J 9 6 4 3　　♢ 9 5　　♣ 10 5

Respond One Heart to One of a minor.

With two four-card suits, normally bid the lower ranking.

♠ K 9 5 3　　♡ K 7 6 5　　♢ Q 5　　♣ 8 4 2

Respond One Heart to One Club or One Diamond. Then you will not miss a fit in either major.

When partner opens a minor suit you may have a choice between supporting him and bidding a major. The decision is swayed by the general strength of the hand and the texture of the two suits.

♠ K J 9 6　　♡ 8 5　　♢ A 7 2　　♣ 10 8 7 3

Bid One Spade over partner's One Club. On the next round you can accord modest support to clubs.

♠ Q 9 8 2　　♡ 10 3　　♢ K J 8 4　　♣ 9 5 3

Now a raise of One Diamond to Two Diamonds is preferred. You are too weak to bid spades and then volunteer support for diamonds, so you show the feature that you know will interest partner.

When one suit is strong and the other weak, bid the strong suit even when it is higher ranking.

♠ A Q 8 7　　♡ 10 6 2　　♢ J 8 6 5　　♣ 9 3

Over partner's One Club show the spades rather than the feathery diamonds.

To respond in a new suit at the Two level requires more strength, at least 8 points. Even then the bid should be avoided on minimum hands unless there is a good five-card suit.

♠ 6 5 2　　♡ J 8 3　　♢ Q 3　　♣ K Q J 6 2

This is just worth Two Clubs over One Spade. Make the clubs slightly weaker and 1NT would be preferable.

♠ 7 3　　♡ K Q 10 6 3 2　　♢ 5　　♣ J 10 6 4

Now 1NT over One Spade would be too unnatural: bid Two Hearts and let the future take care of itself.

2. Medium hands

The responder is most happily placed when he can present a picture of his hand in a single encouraging bid.

Double raise of partner's suit

Double raises, both of a major and a minor, are natural and non-forcing.

(1)	♠ A 5	♡ Q 9 6 2	◇ K J 7 3	♣ J 6 5
(2)	♠ 7	♡ K Q 4	◇ 10 7 6 4 3	♣ A J 8 2

These are average hands for a double raise of One Heart. It will be noted that a well-placed additional Queen would put either hand within the range of an opening bid and a double raise would then be inadequate; that will serve as a guide on many hands. While a double raise generally contains four trumps there is no rule about it and Three Hearts is certainly better than Two Diamonds on hand (2).

A double raise in a minor has a slightly higher limit than in a major because it is sometimes prudent to underbid a little in order not to go beyond 3NT.

♠ 10 3   ♡ A 6 3   ◇ A Q 9 8 5   ♣ J 9 4

If the diamonds were spades you would raise One Spade to Four Spades. You raise One Diamond only to Three.

2NT response

This is a straightforward non-forcing bid, generally made on 11 or 12 points, exceptionally 10 with good intermediates or a barren 13.

2NT, when the values are present, is one of the best bids in the game, much to be preferred to approach bids on hands of no-trump type.

♠ K J 7 3   ♡ Q 10 8   ◇ Q 5   ♣ A 9 8 4

Over One Heart respond 2NT, not One Spade or Two Clubs. If

you have absorbed from other books the notion that you must always show a four-card major you are some distance from being an Acol player.

♠ A 4 3　　　♡ J 10　　　◇ 9 8 7 4　　　♣ A K 6 3

Here, by contrast, is a hand better adapted to suit play. Bid Two Clubs over One Heart – not 2NT just because you have the points.

Response in a new suit

When suits are of unequal length it is usual to bid the longer first even when this means responding at the range of Two.

♠ A K J 2　　　♡ J 5　　　◇ K 10 6 4 3　　　♣ 9 5

Respond Two Diamonds to One Heart, continue with Two Spades over Two Hearts.

With two five-card suits the higher ranking is preferred.

♠ Q 9 7 5 4　　　♡ 8　　　◇ A K J 6 4　　　♣ 10 3

Respond One Spade equally to One Heart or One Club.

When he has only four-card suits the responder has to take careful thought for the future. The best way to tackle this subject is by way of individual examples, for as soon as one begins to formulate principles, reservations and exceptions come to mind.

♠ A J 9 7　　　♡ K 7 5 3　　　◇ K 10 4　　　♣ J 2

Although the spades are better than the hearts you would respond One Heart to One Club so as not to miss a fit in either major. Over a rebid of Two Clubs or Two Hearts you continue with 2NT, not Two Spades.

♠ K Q 9 7　　　♡ A K 6 2　　　◇ 10 7　　　♣ 5 3 2

On this hand you want to show both suits, for both are strong and you have no other feature. Respond One Spade to One Diamond or One Club and show the hearts on the next round.

♠ A Q 5 2　　　♡ 9 6 5　　　◇ 10 4　　　♣ A K 7 2

Over One Diamond, Two Clubs is more far-sighted than One Spade. Suppose that partner rebids Two Diamonds: then you go Two Spades, still aiming at 3NT, and if partner puts you back to

Three Clubs, doubtless supposing that you have five, you can transfer to Three Diamonds. Suppose, on the other hand, that the bidding begins One Diamond – One Spade – Two Diamonds: now Three Clubs is open to the objection that partner may give you Three Spades on J x or x x x, and you will therefore have to gamble an undignified 3NT with no heart guard.

♠ 9   ♡ A Q 8 6   ◇ K 10 4 2   ♣ K 9 7 5

With more than one suit that can be bid at the Two level, the usual practice is to bid the lowest ranking. So, over One Spade, respond Two Clubs, giving partner an easy opportunity to bid either of the other suits.

It follows from this last example that a response of Two Hearts to One Spade will seldom be based on a four-card suit. It should be avoided on any hand that is not well adapted to play in hearts, for partner will often raise on less than normal trump support (see next chapter).

♠ 10 8 6   ♡ A J 7 5   ◇ 7 5 4   ♣ A Q 9

Over One Spade respond Two Clubs. Partner will place you with a club suit but you should be able to take care of future developments. For example, if partner were to raise clubs you could return to Three Spades on your 10 8 6, for he would scarcely ever adopt this sequence with only a four-card spade suit.

Because of the tendency to make the more economical response when only four-card suits are held, there are certain sequences that suggest a five-card suit. We have already mentioned One Spade – Two Hearts. Of the same kind are One Diamond – Two Clubs, and One Heart – Two Diamonds.

3. Strong hands

Under this heading we include all hands on which the responder expects to reach game even if the opener shows no additional strength. For the most part these will be hands that are themselves as good as an opening bid. It is a fair proposition that an opening bid opposite an opening bid should produce game.

Raise of partner's suit

The 'opening bid' test does not apply, of course, to hands containing excellent support for partner's suit. The following qualifies on values for a raise of One Heart to Four.

♠ 8   ♡ K Q 8 5 4   ◇ Q 10 7 6 4 2   ♣ 9

So that partner can distinguish between a raise based on distribution and a raise based more on high cards, the following system is used:

(1) A direct raise, One Spade – Four Spades, may be mainly pre-emptive and in any case will not contain more than 10 or 11 points.

(2) Hands containing the values for an opening bid, about 12 to 14 points, are expressed by a simple response at the range of Two, followed by a jump to game on the next round.

(3) More powerful hands call for a jump shift on the first round. (But see Chapter 13 for a more sophisticated use of this sequence in conjunction with the Swiss Convention.

The following hands illustrate the border between these three courses of action:

(1)   ♠ K J 10 2   ♡ A 8 3   ◇ 7   ♣ Q 9 6 5 2

A maximum, in terms of high cards, for One Spade – Four Spades.

(2)   ♠ K J 10 2   ♡ Q 10 7 4   ◇ A 9   ♣ A 8 2

A maximum delayed game raise (when the Swiss Convention is not in use). Over One Spade or One Heart respond Two Clubs and jump to game in the major on the next round.

(3)   ♠ K J 10 2   ♡ Q 10 7 4   ◇ A Q   ♣ A 8 2

Force with Three Clubs over One Spade or One Heart.

3NT response

This response was described in an earlier book as the 'most stultifying bid in the game' and it has not grown any more beautiful with the years. Since it makes such extravagant use of bidding space and leaves partner with so little room in which to manoeuvre, it should be restricted to balanced hands of notrump type ranging from a good 13 to 15 points.

♠ J 8 2   ♡ K J 7   ◇ K J 4 2   ♣ K Q 9

A typical 3NT response to One Spade.

♠ K 5   ♡ A Q 7   ◇ Q J 3   ♣ K 10 8 7 4

Over One Club there is no better call than 3NT and this would not be a bad response to One Diamond; but over One Spade or One Heart bid a normal Two Clubs.

♠ A 8 3   ♡ K 4   ◇ Q J 7 6   ♣ A 10 9 4

If you respond 3NT to One Spade or One Heart you may well do no harm, but the bid cannot gain as compared with Two Clubs. On the other hand, there will be times when you can arrive at a delicate slam only by the approach route and that is the objection to the 3NT response.

Response in a new suit

With up to 15 or 16 points and no special distribution, a simple response at the level of One or Two will generally be in order. Thus in the present section we shall be considering stronger hands that are good enough for a force or nearly so.

The normal minimum for a jump shift is about 16 points but the bid is made on less when there is strong support for partner or when responder has a powerful suit of his own.

♠ A J 9 3   ♡ 5   ◇ A K 10 5 4 2   ♣ 7 3

Worth Three Diamonds over One Spade but only Two Diamonds over One Heart. Over One Club, One Diamond is sufficient.

♠ A K J 9 7 3   ♡ 6 4   ◇ A Q 2   ♣ 10 5

Worth a force over any One bid.

♠ Q 7   ♡ A Q 6 5   ◇ K 8 4   ♣ A J 10 8

This balanced type of 16-point hand represents a minimum force.

When the decision appears to be borderline the test is not how many points you have, nor how many cards in partner's suit, nor how strong is your own suit, but whether, if you fail to force, you may have an impossible bid on the next round. Take one of the hands above:

♠ A K J 9 7 3   ♡ 6 4   ◇ A Q 2   ♣ 10 5

Suppose that you respond only One Spade to an opening of One Heart and partner on the next round bids Two Diamonds. What then? You can keep the bidding alive with Three Clubs but that won't help to describe your hand. If you jump to Four Spades you will miss a slam whenever partner has three or four right cards.

♠ 9 5   ♡ A K J 8 2   ◇ K J 6   ♣ K 6 3

Here again, if you don't force over One Diamond you will have no satisfactory bid on the next round in many cases; you will be obliged to bid the fourth suit (see Chapter 8).

The next two hands show the opposite side of the picture:

♠ 10   ♡ A 10 5   ◇ K Q 7 3   ♣ A Q 7 4 3

Responding to One Spade you need time to show your various features. No rebid over Two Clubs will embarrass you, for Three Diamonds on the next round will be a natural force.

♠ K 10 8 4   ♡ J   ◇ A J 6 3   ♣ A K 8 3

In the same way, over One Heart a simple Two Clubs is best. The structure of the hand is such that you can cope with any development, and partner's rebid over Two Clubs will be more informative than over a jump shift.

Note that in the last example there was no thought of bidding either One Spade or Two Spades. It is bad in principle to bid weak suits on good hands and that is especially true for forcing responses. It is obvious, for example, that ♠ A x x x opposite ♠ J x x x may be an adequate trump suit for game but is useless for slam.

♠ A 7 5 3   ♡ K 6   ◇ A 10 5 2   ♣ A K J

Over One Heart force with Three Clubs rather than with Two Spades or Three Diamonds. If spades or diamonds are supported you will always be worried that the trump suit may not be good enough. Better, therefore, to give partner the chance to introduce one of those suits. If he raises clubs – which is relatively unlikely – you can play in hearts or notrumps.

Similarly, when forcing on the strength of trump support, choose a suit in which you have first or second round control.

♠ K 2   ♡ A J 8 7   ♢ A K 5   ♣ Q 10 7 3

Over One Heart force with Three Diamonds. That is better than Three Clubs for two reasons: you save partner from worrying about diamonds and you lessen the danger of reaching Six Hearts with two losing clubs in each hand.

4. Jump shift by passed hand

A player who has passed originally will seldom be able to leap forward unless he has a fit for the suit that partner has opened. The jump shift after a pass is therefore treated, not as a vague affirmation of strength, but as a guarantee of a good fit in the opener's suit plus a useful side suit. The bid is forcing for one round only: it is up to the opener to bid game if he has more than a minimum or if his hand is improved by the knowledge that partner has values in a particular side suit.

♠ K 8 5 4   ♡ 6 3   ♢ A Q 8 4 3   ♣ 9 5

After two passes partner opens One Spade. You bid Three Diamonds, showing spade support and good diamonds. If partner can bid only Three Spades you pass. Say that partner has:

(1)   ♠ A Q 9 2   ♡ A 8   ♢ K 10 5   ♣ 10 7 4 2

A minimum opening, but the trump honours and the fit in diamonds enable him to bid Four Spades.

(2)   ♠ A Q J 10 6   ♡ K Q 7   ♢ 9 5 2   ♣ Q 8

A better hand in some ways but the diamond holding is unfavourable and the strength in trumps may be superfluous; so, sign off in Three Spades.

(3)   ♠ A J 9 2   ♡ A K 5   ♢ 9 2   ♣ K 7 6 3

No special fit for diamonds, but since responder has shown the values for a raise to Three Spades the high cards justify a rebid of four Spades.

The opener will sometimes have a chance to make a trial bid of his own.

West	East
♠ 10 6 4	♠ 8
♡ A J 8 7 3	♡ Q 9 5 2
◇ K J 2	◇ A 7 3
♣ Q 5	♣ K J 8 4 3

The bidding goes:

West	East
—	No
1 ♡	3 ♣
3 ◇	4 ♡

Note that if East's diamonds and spades were reversed the contract would be unattractive.

There is nothing to stop responder making this jump shift after passing, even when he has the values for a direct game bid. For example:

♠ K 10 9 4	♡ 6	◇ A 7 4 3 2	♣ K 9 3

Over partner's third- or fourth-hand opening of One Spade you are good enough for Four. So you force with Three Diamonds and if he signs off in Three Spades you still give him Four.

A new suit at the Four level, in such a sequence as No Bid – One Spade – Three Diamonds – Four Clubs, is always a slam suggestion. At the level of Three it may be only a game try.

The first round of bidding is exploratory. Opening bids of One have a wide range and so have all changes of suit in response. But the second round is not too soon to bring the picture into focus. Think of it in this way: On the first round you put out a feeler: if the response is favourable you clinch the deal on the second round: if the response is non-committal you clarify your own position in the hope of reaching early agreement.

Thus on the second round you choose, when reasonably possible, one of the many rebids that define your hand within narrow limits. Do not imagine that it is stylish to make a series of approach bids in preference to a single descriptive bid.

There are four possible kinds of rebid and you will find that three are specifically limit bids.

Rebid in notrumps

The most descriptive bid of all, showing the point count and the balanced distribution.

Raise of responder's suit

In Acol all direct raises are limit bids expressing the full strength of the hand.

Rebid in opener's suit

Again an expression of values, though less accurate than the others because the rebids of Two and Three have to cover a wide range of hands.

Change of suit

This is for hands – there are many of them, of course – that require further development and exploration. A simple change of suit covers a wide but by no means endless field. A jump bid in a new suit is forcing to game.

So the basic principle is this: If there is a convenient way of limiting your hand by making one of the first three types of rebid, choose it. If not, change the suit and declare yourself more precisely on the next round.

We apply that test to various auctions in the following order:

1. Responder bids One over One.
2. Responder bids at the range of Two.
3. Responder makes a Jump Shift.
4. Responder raises your suit.
5. Responder bids Notrumps.

1. Responder bids One over One

Ask yourself first, what is partner's minimum? Normally 6 points, is it not? Base your rebid on that assumption. If he is stronger, that will appear in due course. If he is weaker, that is primarily his responsibility. Certainly you must not, in Acol, employ the so-called 'lee-way principle', whose effect is that the opener carries on his own shoulders the responsibility for every advance. It is hard to establish a satisfactory relationship with a partner whom you assume to be worthless until he bids a second time.

Rebid in notrumps

In general, 22–23 points in the two hands is the mark for 2NT, 25–26 for 3NT, with 24 the boundary line. When there is a vision of 33 points or more, then 6NT should be playable.

In estimating any hand for notrumps, the fit in long suits, controls and good intermediates are all elements that may make a hand play above its value in terms of points. It is contended by some (the professional name is the Theory of Dispersion) that an even distribution of points between the two hands – 12 opposite 12 as against 20 opposite 4 – is an asset. More certain is that 3NT is a good deal easier to make when the majority of the outstanding strength is known to lie with one defender.

As was explained in Chapter 1, the standard for a rebid of 1NT varies according to vulnerability. Not vulnerable, the rebid indicates a balanced hand too strong for an opening 1NT; the range for the rebid is 15–16. Vulnerable, the rebid indicates a balanced hand in the 12–14 range, not strong enough for an opening 1NT.

On fair balanced hands 1NT should be preferred to repetition of a five-card suit.

♠ Q 2   ♡ J 9 5   ◊ A K J 6 3   ♣ K 10 4

Vulnerable, open 1NT. Not vulnerable, open One Diamond and rebid 1NT over a response of One Heart or One Spade.

A rebid in notrumps is sometimes the best choice even with a six-card suit.

♠ K 7   ♡ 6 3   ◊ A J 7   ♣ K Q J 8 5 3

After One Club – One Heart, Two Clubs is inadequate, Three Clubs flamboyant. Not vulnerable, 1NT, suggesting a better than minimum opening, is the best solution.

For a rebid of 2NT you need from a good 16 up to 18 points, for 3NT about 19 or 20. Note that these figures match with the presumption that partner's normal minimum is 6.

Raise of responder's suit

If your hand lends itself to a raise of partner's major to the level of Two, Three or Four, you will seldom need to consider an alternative.

♠ A J 8 7   ♡ 10 9 6 2   ◊ 5   ♣ A Q 10 6

After One Club by you, One Heart by partner, don't start a voyage round the world in eighty bids: express your hand with a raise to Two Hearts. Suppose that you hold:

♠ K 8 2   ♡ 7   ◊ A 10 6 4 3   ♣ K Q 9 8

After One Diamond – One Spade, raise to Two Spades. If you had the Ace of clubs instead of the King, Two Clubs would be in order as you would be strong for Two Spades.

How do you judge whether your hand is worth a raise to Two,

Three or Four? That is not quite our province in this book, for we are concerned more with style and tactics than with basic valuation. We do, however, advise players to cultivate their own judgement and not rely on artificial counts.

Relying on judgement, at least you will learn from your mistakes. When in genuine doubt, relate your hand to a minimum opening. Can you take away a full trick, and so on, and still have an opening and a support?

♠ K Q 7 5　　♡ A K 4　　◇ 9 6　　♣ A Q J 4

West	East
1 ♣	1 ♠
?	

What are you worth now? Take away ♡ A K and you would still have the material for an opening bid and a raise. So, with those two certain tricks, you have enough for Four Spades. Take away the King of hearts and you have a sound raise to Three. Now make the hearts K x x, so that the hand reads:

♠ K Q 7 5　　♡ K 4 3　　◇ 9 6　　♣ A Q J 4

You are on the borderline between a raise to Two Spades and to Three. On such hands we advise: Bid one higher when the trumps are strong, one lower when the hand is good but the trumps moderate. So, on this hand stretch a trifle to Three Spades.

Note that you mustn't be too much affected by your point count when you raise partner.

♠ 10 5 3　　♡ A Q 6 2　　◇ 6　　♣ A K 10 9 4

After One Club – One Heart, bid Three Hearts. If you apply the test mentioned above you will agree that if the hand were 5–4–2–2 it would still be a healthy raise to Two.

♠ Q J 4　　♡ K J 6　　◇ A J　　♣ K J 8 7 5

Here you have 16 points, generally outside the range of a minimum rebid, but after One Club – One Spade, or One Club – One Heart, you are worth only a single raise. (Not vulnerable, you might rebid 1NT.)

When partner responds in a minor suit there is not the same virtue in a direct raise. A more constructive bid, tending towards a major suit or notrumps, will usually be better.

♠ K J 7 3　　♡ 8　　◇ K J 4　　♣ A Q 8 5 2

After One Club – One Diamond, bid One Spade rather than raise diamonds.

Rebid in opener's suit

When an Acol player makes a light tactical opening it is usually because he has a long, strong suit. Such hands are expressed by a minimum rebid in the long suit and it is therefore undesirable in principle to make the same rebid on hands that are more than a Queen or so better than a minimum in high cards. We have noted already that 1NT should be preferred on comparatively balanced hands. If that call would be inapt you may have to improvise.

♠ A Q J   ♡ 8 5 3   ♢ A K J 6 5   ♣ 6 3

After One Diamond – Two Clubs there is no alternative to Two Diamonds. After One Diamond – One Heart it is better to invent a bid of One Spade.

On moderate hands where the choice is between a rebid of the first suit and the introduction of a weak second suit, the question you should put to yourself is: Did I open this minimum hand because I had one good suit or because I had some sort of two-suiter?

♠ 7   ♡ K J 10 6 4 3   ♢ 9 8   ♣ A J 7 2

After One Heart – One Spade bid Two Hearts, for the hearts were the reason why you opened at all. But do not draw from this the conclusion that when you have a minimum opening you must always repeat your suit.

♠ 10   ♡ A K 6 5 2   ♢ 10 8 7   ♣ K J 10 4

You open this hand because you have a flexible 5–4–3–1 with your high cards in the long suits. So, after One Heart – One Spade, rebid Two Clubs. There are few more destructive habits than rebidding the original suit simply to show weakness.

A jump rebid at the Three level (still after a One-over-One beginning) is strong but not forcing. It denotes about six or seven playing tricks and at least a trick better than a minimum in high cards.

♠ Q 9   ♡ A 4   ♢ 9 5   ♣ K Q J 8 4 3 2

Although this hand could be assessed at seven playing tricks we do not advise a jump rebid of Three Clubs. That would bring too wide a range of hands within the scope of this particular bid. It is true that Two Clubs would be an understatement in respect of playing values but that is unlikely to matter since someone at the table will surely bid again.

The following is about a minimum for a jump rebid of Three in a minor, after One Diamond – One Heart:

♠ A 8   ♡ 10 4   ◇ A K Q 10 8 3   ♣ Q 8 6

This is a promising hand for 3NT, but one wants partner to have a bolster, or at least some length, in the unbid suits. With equivalent values and some strength in the unbid suits the opener should rebid 2NT rather than Three Diamonds, even though a little short in points.

Jump rebids in a major suit can be made on a wider range of hands, for now you are within closer reach of game.

♠ K 7   ♡ A J 10 8 6 4   ◇ A Q 2   ♣ 9 3

West	East
1 ♡	1 ♠
3 ♡	

West has only about six playing tricks, but the King of spades is well situated and the hand is certainly too strong for Two Hearts. Exchange the hearts and diamonds and you have an awkward hand for the system in that you have to rebid Two Diamonds on a hand above the normal limit for that call.

A jump rebid at the Four level – uncommon in a minor suit – shows the same type of hand as above, slightly stronger in playing tricks.

Change of suit by opener

We have already noted that introducing a new suit at the minimum level is not in itself a sign of strength. The sequence One Heart – One Spade – Two Diamonds can be made on quite a good hand but also on a minimum two-suiter. Fair strength is guaranteed only when a second suit of higher rank than the first is bid at the Two level. That is the sequence commonly known as a 'reverse'.

♠ K 5   ♡ A Q J 8   ◇ K Q 9 6 2   ♣ 7 6

This 15-point hand is dead minimum for the sequence One Diamond – One Spade – Two Hearts.

Exceptional distribution may compensate for lack of high cards. You need not be nervous of reversing on:

♠ 10   ♡ K Q 9 7 4   ◇ 4   ♣ A K 10 8 4 2

That a reverse should show better than a minimum opening is simply a consequence of the fact that if partner is weak and wants to show minimum preference for the first suit he has to go to the level of Three. That, therefore, is the test: shall I be in trouble if partner is weak and prefers the first suit?

Some systems approach this matter differently. With a strong hand the opener so organizes the bidding that he will be able to make a reverse bid on the second round. That is a playable method but it is not Acol and does not conform with the basic assumption that partner is bidding his cards as he sees them. Do not, therefore, make a 'thing' of reverse bidding: if you can bid your hand in a natural way with reasonable precision, do so.

When the choice is between giving jump support to partner's major and bidding a second suit, a sound principle is to raise the major when four trumps are held but to change the suit with only three-card support.

♠ 6   ♡ K J 8   ◇ A J 10 5 3   ♣ K Q 10 7

West	East
1 ◇	1 ♡
?	

If you had to raise the hearts now, Three Hearts would be about the mark but it might lead to the wrong contract. Better, therefore, to approach with Two Clubs, taking the view that if this is passed Four Hearts can hardly be lay-down.

The only way to force after a One-over-One response is to jump in a new suit.

♠ A J 9 2   ♡ 10   ◇ A K J 4 3   ♣ A K J

West	East
1 ◇	1 ♡
?	

Bid Two Spades. It is a mistake to bid One Spade on the

grounds that 'partner won't pass this One-over-One'. Perhaps he will, but that is not the main objection. Nothing is gained by holding back at this point: you will have to jump later if not now. Furthermore, it puts a strain on other sequences if such a strong hand is not proclaimed by a force. It is fundamental to good bidding that too wide a range of hands should not be shown by the same sequence. It is because they don't appreciate that simple point that American players give themselves so many headaches in the bidding.

In general, you should force whenever game is certain and a direct game bid would not be ideal either because you are too strong or because you may hit on the wrong contract.

♠ Q J 10 7   ♡ K Q 3   ◇ A K J 2   ♣ K 5

West	East
1 ◇	1 ♡
2 ♣	

You have the points for 3NT over One Heart, but either Four Hearts or Four Spades might be better.

♠ A Q 7 2   ♡ 5   ◇ A 10 2   ♣ A K J 10 6

West	East
1 ♣	1 ♠
3 ◇	

This time you know already that spades will be the final contract and you are strong enough for Four. You might as well take a free kick and tell partner that you have a diamond feature and, by inference when you subsequently support spades, that you are short in hearts.

2. Responder bids at the range of Two

The choice of rebid is guided by the same principles as before: if you can find a bid that is limited and descriptive, that will be the best bid. Prefer it to any that is tentative, exploratory or circumambient.

Rebid in notrumps

Partner's response at the level of Two, you will recall, promises at least 8 points, usually more. A rebid of 2NT shows a fairly balanced hand, better than minimum, in the 15–17 range.

♠ K J 4　　　♡ A K 10 7 2　　　◇ A J 9　　　♣ 7 2

After One Heart – Two Clubs, rebid 2NT.

Don't be shy about making this bid on hands that contain a second suit of some kind.

♠ A J 9 8 3　　　♡ A J 8　　　◇ K Q 7 3　　　♣ 10

After One Spade – Two Clubs, 2NT is much more purposeful than Two Diamonds. And if it were four hearts and three diamonds we would still rebid 2NT and take the blame once in twenty times when it turned out badly. Meanwhile we shall often gain in the play at notrumps through concealing the useful major.

A rebid of 3 NT after a Two level response shows from a good 17 to an unslamlike 20. This, too, is a *good* bid: don't stop at the way-side to pick up such uninteresting daisies as K J 9 x in a second suit.

Raise of responder's suit

The main difference (compared with raising a response at the One level) is that trump support does not have to be so good. Partner will usually have a five-card suit; if not, then he will have sufficient all-round strength to take care of the future.

♠ A Q 8 3 2　　　♡ 5 4　　　◇ K 10 6　　　♣ A J 8

West	East
1 ♠	2 ♣
3 ♣	

You would not be out of order in rebidding the spades – indeed, if partner's response were Two Hearts you would have no alternative – but Three Clubs is a more descriptive bid. It does, in fact, suggest five spades, for on most hands containing four clubs and four spades One Club is the better opening.

♠ A K 10 4　　　♡ K J　　　◇ 8 6 5 3　　　♣ A 9 2

Now, after One Spade – Two Hearts, Three Hearts is the best choice. As we have noted above, a response of Two Hearts generally means a five-card suit since with only four-card suits partner will normally respond in the lowest-valued.

A double raise, One Heart – Two Clubs – Four Clubs, should be played as forcing.

Rebid in opener's suit

It is not good thinking to choose a weakish rebid whenever you hold a weakish hand. Do not, therefore, repeat your suit when there is another feature that can be shown without exaggerating your values. We saw an example of that a moment ago when the raise to Three Clubs was preferred to a rebid of the spades. This is another:

♠ A K 9 7 5   ♡ 7 4   ◇ A J 8 3   ♣ 9 6

After One Spade – Two Hearts there is no alternative to Two Spades since the hand is not strong enough for a new suit at the range of Three. After One Spade – Two Clubs the diamonds should be introduced.

The requirements for a jump rebid can be lowered a little when partner has responded at the range of Two.

♠ K 8   ♡ A J 10 7 6 2   ◇ A 9 3   ♣ Q 8

Here the opener could rebid only Two Hearts over a response of One Spade, but he is worth Three Hearts over Two Diamonds or Two Clubs. This jump rebid is not forcing, though partner will surely bid again unless his first response was below standard.

Change of suit

When partner has responded at the Two level it is usual, especially in tournament play, to treat a change of suit as forcing for one round. This is sensible because the combined values must justify a contract of 2NT or higher. The advantage appears when the opener holds a useful hand which may require time for development.

♠ A 4   ♡ A K 7 5 2   ◇ K 8 3   ♣ Q J 4

After One Heart – Two Clubs the opener has no need to plunge into 3NT. He bids simply Two Diamonds, and partner's action over this will be enlightening.

When it is understood that a simple change of suit is forcing for one round, a jump shift will signify support for partner's suit.

♠ A K J 4 2   ♡ A 10 5   ◇ K J 7 3   ♣ 4

After One Spade – Two Diamonds opener rebids Three Hearts. At one stroke he shows strong support for diamonds, a control in hearts, and probably a shortage in clubs.

The requirements for a reverse are less when partner has responded at the Two level.

♠ J 7   ♡ K Q 8 4   ◇ A K 7 4 3   ♣ Q 6

Not vulnerable, open One Diamond, proposing to reverse over Two Clubs or to rebid 1NT over One Spade. Vulnerable, it would be good anticipation to open One Heart, because the sequence One Diamond – One Spade would create a rebid problem.

A new suit at the range of Three is forcing for two rounds. The lower limit is slightly higher than for a reverse.

♠ Q 2   ♡ A K 9 8 4   ◇ J 7   ♣ K Q 5 4

After One Heart – Two Diamonds the right bid is 2NT. Make ·the Jack of diamonds the King and Three Clubs would be in order.

This bid at the range of Three is often used as a strength-showing manoeuvre on a three-card suit. It is a valuable method on hands of the following kind:

♠ A Q 10 8 7   ♡ 5 3   ◇ A 10 6   ♣ A K 5

You open One Spade and partner bids Two Diamonds. Three Clubs is safe and convenient.

3. Responder makes a Jump Shift

When partner forces, his strength is unlimited and a slam is always possible. Considerations of bidding space alter the whole scheme of rebids. Except when he rebids notrumps, it is rarely that the opener will make a bid that precisely limits his hand. He may make the same bid on a minimum or on a good hand with which he intends to proceed to slam.

Rebid in notrumps

The general principle is to rebid as you would have done over a simple response, but necessarily one range higher. Thus, One Diamond – Two Hearts – 2NT suggests initially the same values as One Diamond – One Heart – 1NT. Similarly One Spade – Three Clubs – 3NT shows the fair hand on which you would have rebid 2NT over Two Clubs.

The sequence One Club – Two Hearts – 3NT is neither a stop bid nor a giant: it shows the same sort of values as the last sequence – about 15 or 16 points.

The sequence One Club – Two Hearts – 2NT may also be adopted for tactical reasons on good hands.

♠ A Q 2   ♡ Q 8 4   ◇ K 5   ♣ A Q 10 5 3

West	East
1 ♣	2 ♡
2NT	

With 17 points and a fit for partner you are now sure to reach a slam. Your best move for the moment is to mark time with 2NT and discover partner's intentions. You mislead him for the moment but his next bid will be none the less illuminating.

Raise of responder's suit

A raise below the game level of partner's jump shift is unlimited: it may be a minimum hand, it may be strong.

The double raise is best reserved for hands containing excellent trump support but otherwise minimum values.

♠ 7 4   ♡ K Q 10 5   ◇ A J 9 5 3 2   ♣ 8

After One Diamond – Two Hearts, raise to Four Hearts. Don't miss an opportunity for this sort of jump raise: it may be the only way to convince partner (with ♡ A x x x x) that there is no hole in his bucket.

Rebid of opener's suit

A simple rebid over a force, like a single raise, is unlimited.

A jump rebid in this and other game-forcing situations denotes a solid suit but, if made at the game level, to some degree limits the hand.

(1) ♠ 6 2   ♡ A K Q J 8 3   ◇ 9 8   ♣ Q J 3

(2) ♠ A 2   ♡ A K Q J 8 3   ◇ 9 8   ♣ Q J 3

On hand (1), after One Heart – Three Diamonds or One Heart – Two Spades, the jump to Four Hearts well expresses the hand. On hand (2), after a similar sequence, the opener will surely be advancing to slam and should bid only Three Hearts for the nonce.

Change of suit

After a jump shift the opener should introduce a second suit without any of the inhibitions that sometimes affect his rebid after a simple response.

♠ A K 9 7 5   ♡ 7 4   ◇ A J 8 3 2   ♣ 9

After One Spade – Two Hearts the opener must bid Two Spades. After One Spade – Three Hearts he can show the diamonds. Similarly, a sequence such as One Club – Two Spades – Three Hearts does not show the values (though it does show the distribution) associated with a reverse.

4. Responder raises your suit

After a single raise the opener should pass a balanced 16 points. A rebid of 2NT suggests 16 with a 5-card suit, or 17–18.

Unbalanced hands that are somewhat better than a minimum are often hard to judge after a single raise. A rebid of Three in the original suit, One Spade – Two Spades – Three Spades, is generally played as slightly less encouraging than a bid of a second suit. An example would be:

♠ A Q 10 7 6 4   ♡ K Q 6   ◇ K 8 3   ♣ 3

Some tournament players treat Three Spades in this sequence as a specifically defensive manoeuvre, designed to prevent an opponent from protecting. Such a method has its advantages in match point play, more especially when the suit is hearts.

When the major-suit opener bids a second suit at the Three level he is said to make a trial bid, encouraging partner to go Four unless his first raise was weak. The trial bid is normally made in a suit where the opener looks for supporting cards or a ruffing value.

♠ A 7   ♡ K Q 10 8 2   ◇ K 4   ♣ K 10 3 2

Here the natural trial bid, after One Heart – Two Hearts, is Three Clubs.

When the opening bid is a minor, the introduction of a major on the second round is a trial bid to the extent that it should not be passed, but responder should allow for the possibility that it may be a genuine suit and should raise with trump support.

(1) ♠ A K 4 2   ♡ A Q 9   ◇ K J 8 7 3   ♣ 5

(2) ♠ 7   ♡ A K J   ◇ A K J 8 6 2   ♣ J 10 7

On hand (1), after One Diamond – Two Diamonds, the opener can explore the possibility of a spade game. On hand (2) he bids Two Hearts as a forward-going move which may lead to 3NT or to Five Diamonds.

Partner raises to the level of Three

While jump raises are not forcing, the opener needs little excuse to bid on. He should pass only on the type of 4–4–3–2 or 5–3–3–2 hand that has to be opened but is decidedly weak in playing tricks For example:

(1) ♠ Q 3   ♡ A K 8 3   ◇ A 9 5 2   ♣ 9 6 3

(2) ♠ A K J 7 2   ♡ 6 5 3   ◇ K 8 6   ♣ J 4

Any new suit after a raise to Three in a major is a slam try. The various manoeuvres are discussed in the chapter on slam bidding.

5. Responder bids Notrumps

Partner responds 1NT and you have a rather weak, unbalanced hand. Do you take out? This is a situation which many players tend to misjudge.

The first point to note is that it is a mistake to remove 1NT simply because you are not happy about it.

♠ A Q 10 5 2   ♡ Q 8 4   ◇ K 8 6 5   ♣ J

West	East
1 ♠	1NT
?	

You may fear a minus score in 1NT but it is still a mistake to remove to Two Spades or to place a toe delicately on Two Diamonds.

Each of these bids is wrong for two reasons. Firstly, although not strength-showing they are forward-going in the sense that they raise the level of the contract. Such an advance should be more than a symptom of discomfort. Secondly, there is no assurance that even if you are allowed to settle in Two Spades or Two Diamonds, as is likely but not certain, you will be improving your prospects of a plus score. Partners who respond 1NT to One Spade are often short of spades and often have four or five cards of the suit in which opener has a singleton.

That last point brings us to the factor that is decisive on these hands: What is the likelihood, on the bidding, of responder having length in the opener's short suits? Compare these two hands:

(1) ♠ K Q J 7 2   ♡ 8 2   ◇ A Q J 6   ♣ J 5

(2) ♠ 9 7   ♡ J 6   ◇ K Q J 7 3   ♣ A Q J 4

On hand (1), after One Spade – 1NT, there are no grounds whatsoever for introducing Two Diamonds. Partner may well have complementary shape – 2–4–2–5. On hand (2), after One Diamond – 1NT, it is right to bid Two Clubs, for partner's failure to respond in either major suggests that he may have six cards in the minors and very likely more. In particular, when partner responds 1NT to One Club, there is a presumption that he has at least three cards in clubs.

Over partner's notrump response, the rebid on balanced hands presents fewer complications. Placing partner with an average 6 to 9 points, the opener will raise to 2NT on 17 or a moderate 18.

A jump in the opener's suit, One Heart – 1NT – Three Hearts, is not forcing. A jump in a new suit, One Heart – 1NT – Three Diamonds, is best played as forcing for one round only. It is difficult otherwise to show strength on a hand of the following kind:

♠ K Q 6   ♡ A Q 8 4 2   ◇ A J 8 7   ♣ 6

The bidding begins: One Heart – 1NT. Now you bid Three Diamonds and if partner can say only Three Hearts you are free to pass.

The rebid over 2NT

Any change of suit is forcing, but not to game. One Spade – 2NT, Three Diamonds – Three Spades, can be passed by the opener.

A minimum rebid of the opener's suit, One Heart – 2NT – Three Hearts, is discouraging in Acol, but here again we warn against advancing the level of the auction simply because you are not content with the present state of affairs.

♠ A J 10 7 4   ♡ 5   ◇ Q 8 2   ♣ K J 8 3

You make a third-hand opening of One Spade and partner obtusely gives you 2NT. You must let him do his best, not bid Three Spades or Three Clubs in the hope that you may find some more comfortable resting-place.

Remember that Three Clubs would be forcing, though on this occasion you would prefer it otherwise.

The rebid over 3NT

While a rebid to Four Hearts or Four Spades means no more than that you prefer that contract to 3NT, Four of a minor suit is constructive and probably a slam attempt.

West	*East*
1 ◇	3NT
4 ◇ (or 4 ♣)	

It is probable that West has slam notions, for otherwise he would have left 3NT. East's choice is to play along with a raise or cue-bid, or to sign off in 4NT.

A jump to Five of a minor would suggest a long suit and few high cards.

♠ 4   ♡ A 3   ◇ Q J 9 6 4 3 2   ♣ K 8 7

After One Diamond – 3NT, bid Five Diamonds.

By the time the fourth bid is reached, the variations are numerous and in this chapter we shall concern ourselves mainly with the forcing or non-forcing quality of responder's second bid. We study these in relation to the opener's rebid in the following order:

1. Opener has rebid 1NT.
2. Opener has rebid 2NT.
3. Opener has rebid 3NT.
4. Opener has raised responder's suit.
5. Opener has made a minimum rebid in his own suit.
6. Opener has made a jump rebid in his own suit.
7. Opener has made a simple change of suit.
8. Opener has made a jump shift.

1. Opener has rebid 1NT
Non-forcing rebids by responder

These rebids are presented, roughly speaking, in order of encouragement.

West	East
1 ◇	1 ♡
1NT	2 ♡

East is limited and West will usually pass.

West	East
1 ◇	1 ♡
1NT	2 ◇

East's return to partner's first suit has a slightly higher upper limit than the return to his own suit, since with a decidedly weak hand he would raise diamonds on the first round.

West	East
1 ♣	1 ♠
1NT	2 ◇

This change of suit could be described as neutral. West does not have to bid again but if he can show preference for spades or raise diamonds it may be that East will try for game.

West	East
1 ♡	1 ♠
1NT	2NT

About 11–12 when vulnerable, 9–10 when not vulnerable. If opener bids again over 2NT, either Three Hearts or Three Spades, this should be treated as forcing.

West	East
1 ◇	1 ♠
1NT	3 ◇

This is strongly invitational, but not forcing. The strength will again depend on vulnerability. Facing a 12–14 rebid, East may be as good as:

♠ A Q 6 5 3   ♡ 9   ◇ K J 8 3   ♣ 10 7 4

As we shall see in the next section, the jump would be forcing if both major suits were involved.

West	East
1 ♣	1 ♡
1NT	3 ♡

Strongly invitational, whether the rebid showed 12–14 or 15–16.

Forcing rebids by responder

West	East
1 ♣	1 ◇
1NT	2 ♠

Any reverse by responder is forcing.

A jump in partner's suit is forcing when both majors have been bid.

West	East
1 ♡	1 ♠
1NT	3 ♡

If Three Hearts is not played as forcing East has no good bid on a hand such as:

♠ K Q 8 4 2   ♡ A J 7   ♢ Q 6   ♣ 7 5 2

He has the values for 3NT but either Four Spades or Four Hearts might be safer.

West	East
1 ♣	1 ♠
1NT	3 ♡

This jump in a new suit over 1NT (as in the comparable sequence, One Heart – 1NT – Three Clubs) is best played as forcing for one round only. East may have a hand of this sort:

♠ A K 10 4 2   ♡ Q 10 7 5 2   ♢ 6   ♣ 8 3

If partner (marked with 12–14) can bid only Three Spades over Three Hearts, East should pass. It follows that West should bid game whenever he has a fair holding in either of partner's suits.

2. Opener has rebid 2NT
Non-forcing rebids by responder

The only discouraging bid is a rebid of the responder's suit.

West	East
1 ♢	1 ♡
2NT	3 ♡

West	East
1 ♡	2 ♣
2NT	3 ♣

In both instances East transmits the message that so far as he can tell game is uncertain. The presumption is that his suit is long but lacking in high cards.

Forcing rebids by responder

A return to the opener's suit, or a bid of a new suit, is forcing for one round.

West	East
1 ♣	1 ♠
2NT	3 ♣

East may be strong but he is also free to pass on the next round if partner can offer nothing more constructive than Three Spades.

West	East
1 ♠	2 ♣
2NT	3 ♠

This is forcing to game in effect.

3. Opener has rebid 3NT

The distinction here is between bids that present no encouragement to slam and bids that are forward-going to a greater or lesser degree.

Bids that present no encouragement

A simple return to responder's major suit is a sign-off.

West	East
1 ◇	1 ♡
3NT	4 ♡

Bids that are forward-going

Apart from the sequence above, the general principle is that one does not *rescue* 3NT. A sequence such as the following is mildly constructive.

West	*East*
1 ♣	1 ♠
3NT	4 ♡

East should not disturb 3NT on ♠ J 10 x x x and ♡ K x x x x. For one thing, it is possible that West's 3NT is largely based on clubs. East should be more like A J x x x and K x x x x in the majors.

A return to partner's major suit is also encouraging.

West	*East*
1 ♡	1 ♠
3NT	4 ♡

Remember that with a weak hand East would probably raise to Two Hearts on the first round. He should have something like:

♠ A Q 6 5 4   ♡ K 7 3   ◇ J 8   ♣ 9 8 7

Bids that are forcing

Four of a minor at this stage is always forcing.

West	*East*
1 ♠	2 ♣
3NT	4 ♣

Since this Four Clubs is constructive the opener may carry the bidding to Six without further encouragement. A jump to Five Clubs over 3NT would suggest a weaker hand.

4. Opener has raised responder's suit
Non-forcing rebids by responder

A return to opener's minor suit at the level of Three is encouraging but not forcing.

West	*East*
1 ◇	1 ♠
2 ♠	3 ◇

East has hopes of game. Something like:

♠ A Q 8 5   ♡ 4 2   ◇ K 10 7 4   ♣ Q 8 4

West should take it as likely that the spades are a four-card suit.
When opener's suit is a major the corresponding sequence is
still not forcing.

West	East
1 ♡	2 ♣
3 ♣	3 ♡

East's general strength will be about the same as for a direct
raise to Three, but the trump support may be no better than
10 x x. A minimum for East would be:

♠ 10 5   ♡ A 9 7   ◇ 7 6 5   ♣ A Q 10 8 2

There is really no other way to bid this hand. Make it a little
stronger and then some other call can be found in place of the non-
forcing Three Hearts:

(1)   ♠ 10 5   ♡ A J 7   ◇ 7 6 5   ♣ A K 10 8 2

(2)   ♠ 7 6   ♡ J 9 7   ◇ A 10 5   ♣ A K 10 8 2

There is a home in our goldfish bowl for any player who is
nervous of Four Hearts on hand (1). On hand (2) Three Diamonds
is the best bid over Three Clubs.

Forcing rebids by responder

A return to partner's suit is forcing in the following circumstances:
    (a) When both majors have been bid (compare One Heart – One
Spade, 1NT – Three Hearts).

West	East
1 ♡	1 ♠
2 ♠	3 ♡

Similarly, One Spade – Two Hearts, Three Hearts – Three
Spades, is forcing.

(b) When responder jumps in a minor.

West	East
1 ◇	1 ♠
2 ♣	4 ◇

It should be assumed that East is prepared for game in one suit or the other.

(c) When there has been a double raise.

West	East
1 ♣	1 ♡
3 ♡	4 ♣

Four Clubs sounds like the beginning of a slam try.

After a single raise a bid in a new suit is a trial bid, forcing for one round.

East holds:

♠ J 8   ♡ K J 8 2   ◇ A Q 9   ♣ Q 10 4 2

West	East
1 ♣	1 ♡
2 ♡	3 ◇

As the hand may play better in 3NT than Four Hearts, East makes a forcing bid to show control of diamonds. He is too strong to bid Three Clubs, which would not be forcing.

5. Opener has made a minimum rebid in his own suit

After a minimum rebid responder's problem is not so much to know what is forcing as to judge when to bid at all and in what denomination.

When responder should pass

Since opener has made a bid that proclaims limited strength, responder should not take out on weakness.

West	East
1 ◇	1 ♠
2 ◇	?

East should pass any of the following hands:

(1)	♠ Q 10 7 6 4 2	♡ K 6 3	◇ 5	♣ J 6 2
(2)	♠ K 9 6 4 3	♡ A 7 5 4 2	◇ 6	♣ 4 3
(3)	♠ K Q 6 4	♡ K J 6	◇ 9 7	♣ 10 8 5 2

On hand (1) East may think he has a better chance of making Two Spades than his partner has of making Two Diamonds, but that is not certain and, as we shall see below, the rebid of responder's suit has to be made on considerably better hands than this.

On hand (2) there is little likelihood of game and East should not suppose that he is obliged to announce his second suit. The bidding may easily go out of control.

On hand (3) East is reasonably well upholstered in the unbid suits, but his lack of Aces or of a supporting card in diamonds leaves him below strength for 2NT.

When responder should raise opener or bid 2NT

Particularly when he rebids his suit over a response at the level of One, thus by-passing 1NT, opener will have a good suit with little strength outside. Good judgement will often manifest itself in support for the suit when some other bid may seem equally attractive.

The bidding goes:

West	East
1 ♡	1 ♠
2 ♡	?

East should raise to Three Hearts on any of the following hands:

(1)	♠ A 9 7 6 4	♡ Q 4	◇ A 6 5	♣ J 6 2
(2)	♠ K J 8 5 4	♡ 10 6	◇ A 7	♣ K 7 4 2
(3)	♠ A Q 6 4 3 2	♡ A 8 .	◇ J 10 2	♣ 7 4

On the first two hands the values are present for 2NT, but owing to the lack of tenaces and intermediates the raise of the suit is better. On hand (3) the choice is nicely balanced, but Two Spades would be a slight underbid and Three Spades does not appeal on such irresolute trumps.

When partner has rebid his suit over a response at the range of Two the inference that he has a one-suited hand is less strong.

♠ A 7   ♡ 10 6   ◇ K J 8 5 4   ♣ K 7 4 2

This is the same hand as (2) above with the suits changed. Now, after One Heart – Two Diamonds – Two Hearts, 2NT is the bid.

When responder should repeat his suit

As we have already noted, responder should not rebid his own suit without constructive purpose.

West	East
1 ◇	1 ♡
2 ◇	2 ♡
———	

These two hands are approximately minimum and maximum hands for that sequence:

(1)   ♠ K 6 5   ♡ K J 10 8 4 2   ◇ 6 2   ♣ 9 8

(2)   ♠ K 6 5   ♡ A K 10 6 5 3   ◇ 6 2   ♣ 9 8

The repeat of a minor suit over a major will always be taken as a request for 3NT and may be as strong as:

♠ 5   ♡ A 8 2   ◇ 9 4 3   ♣ A Q J 9 7 4

After One Spade – Two Clubs – Two Spades, East has no good alternative to Three Clubs.

A jump rebid by responder is not forcing but it sometimes has to be made on a very useful hand.

West	East
1 ♣	1 ♠
2 ♣	3 ♠
———	

East's hand should be as good as an opening bid and he can have as much as A K J x x x with a side Ace. West should pass only if he has a tactical opening, unsuitable for spades.

Non-forcing changes of suit by responder

A simple change of suit that allows opener to return to the first suit at the level of Two is constructive but not forcing.

West	East
1 ♣	1 ♠
2 ♣	2 ♡
	——

As we noted at the beginning of this section, East should not introduce the new suit just because he is unhopeful of Two Clubs: he is inviting partner to bid again.

Forcing changes of suit by responder

A reverse by responder, or a new suit at the range of Three, is forcing for one round. Since it will not be left in and will not normally be raised on less than four trumps, this type of bid is often made by anglers for 3NT.

West	East
1 ♣	1 ◇
2 ♣	2 ♠
	——

East may have a two-suiter or he may have a hand of this kind:

♠ A K 2   ♡ 9 5   ◇ K 10 8 4 3   ♣ J 10 6

Even if he holds four spades, opener will not normally raise the second suit beyond the Three level.

6. Opener has made a jump rebid in his own suit

After a jump rebid by the opener any bid below the game level is forcing.

West	East
1 ♣	1 ♡
3 ♣	3 ♡
	——

East may be no better than:

♠ 10 3 2   ♡ K Q 10 9 6   ◇ 7 4 3   ♣ Q 5

He may also have a good hand, however, and be marking time. A raise to Four Clubs would also be forcing.

When he rebids a minor at the range of Four responder must be strong.

West	East
1 ♡	2 ◇
3 ♡	4 ◇

East is prepared for game at least. If he has a weak hand with long diamonds he must pass Three Hearts.

7. Opener has made a simple change of suit
When responder is weak

When the opener changes the suit his upper limit is about 18 points. Responder should usually find a second bid on 7 points. These are hands on which he should pass:

West	East
1 ♣	1 ♡
1 ♠	No

(1)   ♠ 7 5 4   ♡ K J 6 4 3   ◇ Q 10 6   ♣ 9 5

East is under strength for 1NT, which on the second round shows about 7 to 10 points.

(2)   ♠ 5 3 2   ♡ K 10 7 5 4 2   ◇ 6 5   ♣ Q 8

East has responded on the first round because of his six-card suit. When that is not supported he must pass and cut his losses.

On very weak hands it is a mistake either to bid 1NT or to give preference.

(3)   ♠ 7 5   ♡ K J 8 3 2   ◇ Q 7 4 3   ♣ 9 2

East should take shelter in a pass before the rains come.

Medium and encouraging bids

A jump to 2NT when partner has rebid at the One level shows the same values as 2NT over an opening bid. When the bidding is already at the Two level responder may have to shade this call.

West	East
1 ♣	2 ♣
2 ♡	?

East holds:

♠ 5 2 ♡ J 10 8 ♢ Q J 3 ♣ K Q 9 8 7

As noted above, opener's change of suit after the response at the range of Two is forcing. This is a little inconvenient for East, whose Two Clubs (in preference to 1NT) was borderline. A shaded 2NT is better than a false preference to Two Spades, as recommended in some systems. In Acol you make the sensible bid without fear of being court-martialled over a deficiency of a point or two.

This is another situation where the responder may have to stretch:

♠ 10 6 ♡ Q 8 3 ♢ A K 7 4 2 ♣ 6 4 2

West	East
1 ♠	2 ♢
2 ♡	?

Better to risk overbalancing with Three Hearts than to leave partner suspended in mid-air.

Jump preference in response to partner's change of suit can freely be given with three-card support. East holds:

♠ A K 8 5 3 ♡ 9 6 4 ♢ J 10 ♣ 8 7 5

West	East
1 ♡	1 ♠
2 ♢	?

If the clubs and diamonds were reversed, Two Hearts would be enough. As things are, West should not count his points but should trust that his diamond holding will be useful.

A jump in responder's suit is non-forcing.

West	East
1 ◇	1 ♠
2 ♣	3 ♠

After opener's change of suit, Two Spades by responder would be quite weak, so Three Spades is simply invitational. East may hold:

♠ A J 10 9 7 3   ♡ 7 3   ◇ A 9   ♣ 8 5 2

If East is stronger he must introduce the fourth suit. See the next section.

Forcing bids by responder

A jump raise in partner's minor suit, One Heart – Two Clubs, Two Diamonds – Four Diamonds, is forcing. It is true that partner's Two Diamonds may be an invented bid, but in that case he will be better than minimum and will have somewhere to go.

For the rest, responder can force only by introducing the fourth suit.

West	East
1 ◇	1 ♠
2 ♣	2 ♡

East holds:

♠ A J 10 9 7 3   ♡ 7 3   ◇ A 9   ♣ K 5 2

This is the same hand as above, with the King of clubs instead of a low club. East intends to reach game now, and to gain time he bids the fourth suit. He will probably have an opportunity on the next round to repeat his spades.

The technique of fourth-suit bidding requires special study and is examined in Chapter 8.

8. Opener has shown reversing values
Non-forcing bids by the responder

There are only three sequences where responder's second bid may close the chapter.

(a) Responder bids 2NT.

West	East
1 ♦	1 ♠
2 ♥	2NT

East may be no stronger than:

♠ Q 10 7 4 3   ♥ 7 5   ♦ 9 8 6   ♣ A J 6

With upwards of 10 points responder should bid 3NT or make some other constructive bid.

(b) A minimum rebid of responder's suit over a reverse at the level of Two.

West	East
1 ♦	1 ♠
2 ♥	2 ♠

or

West	East
1 ♦	2 ♣
2 ♠	3 ♣

(c) A minimum return to partner's minor suit at the range of Three.

West	East
1 ♣	1 ♠
2 ♥	3 ♣

Forcing bids by responder

The main reason for defining the following sequences as forcing is to gain space for the exploration of alternative game contracts.

(a) A return to hearts at the level of Three.

West	East
1 ♡	2 ♣
2 ♠	3 ♡
—	—

It is seldom that West would want to stay one short of game at this point. On the other hand, there are many occasions where the correct denomination may be in doubt. Suppose East holds:

♠ 10 9 4   ♡ Q 7   ◇ A 6 2   ♣ A 10 8 7 3

Now the forcing quality of Three Hearts gives scope for nice judgement. Another advantage is that Four Hearts can be used as a slam suggestion.

♠ J 7   ♡ Q 10 4   ◇ K 9 4   ♣ A K 6 5 2

On this hand East jumps to Four. With a low heart instead of the Queen he would bid only Three, for any slam suggestion must come from his partner.

(b) A raise to Three of partner's second suit.

West	East
1 ◇	1 ♠
2 ♡	3 ♡
—	—

Very occasionally it may suit the partnership to stop at this level, but more often East will want to make a bid that leaves various possibilities open. One Club – One Heart, Two Diamonds – Three Diamonds, is similarly forcing.

(c) Any kind of jump bid below the game level.

West	East
1 ♣	1 ♡
2 ◇	3 ♡
—	—

East may not be strong when he makes this bid, but since it is unrealistic to suppose that the bidding may die it is best to classify the jump as forcing. That can be convenient when East has slam notions.

West	East
1 ◇	1 ♠
2 ♡	4 ◇
—	—

Here, again, East may not always be strong but when he has a good hand he must be free to jump without fear that the bidding may stop.

(d) Any bid after the opener has bid at the level of Three.

West	East
1 ♡	2 ◇
3 ♣	3 ◇ or 3 ♡

The theory here is that the opener should not bid a new suit at the Three level unless he is willing to bid once more. The advantage – that responder does not have to make a precipitous jump every time he is better than a minimum – is seen on this type of hand:

West	East
1 ♠	2 ♡
3 ♣	3 ♡

East holds:

♠ Q 5   ♡ K Q 9 8 5 3   ◇ 9 4 3   ♣ K 8

East has enough for Four Spades if no safer contract presents itself, but hearts may be superior. Unless Three Hearts is recognized as forcing there is no sure way of arriving at the better contract.

9. Opener has made a jump shift

When the opener forces on the second round he usually has values in responder's suit. Responder should rebid his suit when possible, in preference to an unhelpful 3NT.

West	East
1 ♡.	1 ♠
3 ◇	?

♠ A J 8 5 2   ♡ 9 4   ◇ J 2   ♣ K 7 4 2

Better Three Spades now than 3NT.

Although there is a forcing situation responder should not

neglect to show extra values by a jump, especially on hands where he cannot himself make the first slam try.

♠ A K 10 2   ♡ Q J 7   ◇ J 2   ♣ J 7 4 2

After the same bidding as above, jump to Four Hearts, showing positive support.

West	East
1 ♣	1 ♡
2 ♠	?

♠ J 7 3   ♡ A Q 4 2   ◇ K J 10   ♣ 8 5 2

If you don't bid 3NT now you may have difficulty later in reflecting your medium all-round values.

In this chapter we discuss opening bids of 1NT, 2NT and 3NT, and the subsequent bidding.

One Notrump opening and responses

The standards we recommend for 1NT openings at rubber bridge are: not vulnerable, 12 to 14 points; vulnerable, 15 to 17 points.

The advantages of a 1NT opening are well known: it is descriptive, limited and awkward to overcall. But in appreciating the virtues one must not be blind to the faults. An opening 1NT is an unreliable springboard for slam bidding, especially when the only good fit is in a minor suit. When partner has not passed you should beware of opening a strong notrump on hands that are fitted to suit play, particularly 4–4–3–2 hands that could well end up in a minor suit slam.

♠ Q 9 7 2   ♡ K 8   ◇ A K 8 4   ♣ A J 3

Open One Diamond first or second in hand, 1NT third or fourth in hand.

We do not propose to renew here the theoretical argument about the merits of playing a weak or strong notrump at different times, but we will remark that one of the advantages of a weak notrump non-vulnerable is that it can be used as a semi-psychic manoeuvre on a wide variety of hands. In almost any position we recommend 1NT on:

♠ J 5   ♡ K 7 2   ◇ A K 10 8 3   ♣ Q 7 5

If you want to be really 'with it' and in third position open a beatnik (long and straggly) notrump on

♠ 9 2   ♡ K J 4   ◇ Q 4   ♣ A 10 8 6 3 2

you will seldom come to harm and will often steal the bid from more powerful opponents.

Strong responses to 1NT

A jump to Three of a suit is a normal force to game.

(1) ♠ K 9 8   ♡ K J 10 6 5   ◇ 7   ♣ A J 6 3

(2) ♠ K 7   ♡ A 4   ◇ A Q 9 6 5 2   ♣ K 10 6

Hand (1) is just worth a force of Three Hearts over a weak no-trump. If partner continues with 3NT you should pass.

Hand (2) is about maximum for a force to game as opposed to a slam try. If partner, over Three Diamonds, bids 3NT you should pass, and over Three of a major you should only bid 3NT. The fact that you have forced in a minor suit is of itself an indication that you are prepared to raise your eyes above game level.

In responding to a force, the notrump bidder should raise the suit whenever he has reasonable support, even when the hand is balanced and all suits are guarded.

♠ Q 9 5   ♡ K 6 4   ◇ A J 7   ♣ Q J 8 7

After 1NT – Three Spades, assume that partner has his reasons and raise to Four Spades.

With a better than average notrump and good support for partner, do not be nervous of signifying that you are willing to share thoughts of a slam.

♠ Q J 5 2   ♡ K J 8   ◇ K 9 4 2   ♣ A 7

After 1NT – Three Spades you should bid Four Clubs, for although you have only one Ace you are maximum in other respects.

Weak responses to 1NT

Two of a suit (other than Two Clubs) is a sign-off, but we advise against disturbing 1NT, whether weak or strong, on hands such as the following:

(1) ♠ J 8 6 5 3   ♡ Q 4   ◇ Q 10 4 2   ♣ 9 6

(2) ♠ 3   ♡ 9 4 2   ◇ K J 8 3 2   ♣ J 7 4 3

(3) ♠ J 10 7 2   ♡ 6   ◇ A 8 6 5 3   ♣ 7 4 2

On hand (1), especially, it is unlikely that playing in the suit will gain you two extra tricks. (If only one trick, there is no point in disturbing 1NT.) With the other hands different considerations arise according to whether the notrump is strong or weak. If strong, you should make 1NT; if weak, perhaps not, but by bidding Two Diamonds you reopen the bidding for the player who passed over 1NT and, if anything, you make it easier for opponents to compete. Contrary to general belief, a pass by the responder to 1NT is often the best intimidating manoeuvre.

The notrump opener will generally pass a simple take-out but he is not debarred from raising (a) if he has a maximum notrump with good support for the suit, or (b) a weak notrump with such support for the suit that a raise seems advisable if only for pre-emptive reasons.

♠ J 4   ♡ A Q J 2   ◇ K 6 3 2   ♣ Q 9 6

Having opened 1NT and received a response of Two Hearts we would advance to Three, at any rate against aggressive opponents.

Two Club response to 1NT

Acol players used this convention long before it became known all over the world as 'Stayman'. In its modern form the convention has two main objects. One is to discover a possible fit in a major suit; the other to increase the accuracy of suit responses to 1NT by supplying, as it were, an extra echelon of bids.

The notrump bidder's duty on the first round is clear-cut: if he has a four-card major he must bid it; if not, he must bid Two Diamonds. In the following sequences the convention is used in search of a fit:

(1)	*West*	*East*
	1NT	2 ♣
	2 ◇	2 ♡ or 2 ♠

East's second bid is a sign-off. The presumption is that he would have been content to play in the other suit had partner so responded.

If West has a doubleton heart and three spades it is logical for him to transfer Two Hearts to Two Spades.

(2) *West*   *East*
    1NT   2 ♣
    2 ♡   2 ♠

Again a sign-off but there is an inference that East would have raised a favourable response of Two Spades.

(3) *West*   *East*
    1NT   2 ♣
    2 ◇, 2 ♡ or 2 ♠   2NT

No fit has been discovered and the sequence is in effect the same as a direct raise to 2NT.

When the notrump bidder has four cards in both majors he should bid Two Hearts and may declare the spades later.

Two Clubs followed by Three Clubs is a sign-off. Two Clubs followed by Three Diamonds is also non-forcing.

In the next group the convention is used not only to discover a fit but also to portray values just short of a force to game.

(1) *West*   *East*
    1NT   2 ♣
    2 ◇   3 ♡ or 3 ♠

(2) *West*   *East*
    1NT   2 ♣
    2 ♡   3 ♠

(3) *West*   *East*
    1NT   2 ♣
    2 ♣   3 ♡

A typical hand for the bid of Three Hearts in examples (1) or (3), after a non-vulnerable opening, would be:

♠ 8   ♡ A 10 7 6 4 2   ◇ K Q 5   ♣ 7 3 2

The opener should regard this sequence as similar in type to 1NT – Three Hearts, but not so strong.

Two Notrump opening and responses

The opening suggests in principle 20 to 22 points, balanced distribution, a guard in every suit. In practice, any of these requirements can be slipped overboard when the weather is otherwise set fair.

(1) ♠ A K Q 10 3   ♡ K 5   ◇ K 2   ♣ A Q 8 3

The fact that you have a set-up major suit is no bar to 2NT: it is a recommendation. The disadvantage of opening Two Spades here is that if partner responds 2NT the final contract may be 3NT played from the wrong side.

(2) ♠ J 7   ♡ A Q 9   ◇ A Q J 4   ♣ A K J 3

Here you have no spade guard and no good suit to run if you lose the first four tricks in spades. However, with 22 points you have too much for an opening One bid and 2NT is the best solution.

(3) ♠ K 4   ♡ Q 10 5   ◇ A K Q 10 7 3   ♣ A 8

This time you have only 18 points but 2NT is the obvious bid, especially if partner has passed. First or second in hand, One Diamond is safer, though we do not say that it is better.

Responses to 2 NT opening

Any suit response at the level of Three is forcing. When responder bids Three Hearts or Three Spades, the opener should generally raise with three-card support. Strong support, or a hand well suited to trump play, can be indicated by an advance cue bid.

♠ K J 10 2   ♡ K Q 2   ◇ A 5   ♣ A K J 3

After 2NT – Three Hearts, don't bid a sleepy Four Hearts! Show that you are in the upper bracket by making a cue-bid of Four Clubs. If partner has no aspirations beyond game he can sign off in Four Hearts.

A jump to Four of a major (2NT – Four Hearts or Four Spades) is best played as a sign-off. It follows that the sequence 1NT – Three Hearts, 3NT – Four Hearts, is a slam suggestion.

Three Clubs over 2NT

Three Clubs over 2NT, like Two Clubs over 1NT, is conventional. If the opener has a four-card major suit he should bid it. Three

Diamonds shows a diamond suit and 3NT, by inference, a club suit. (Some players prefer the Baron method, whereby opener bids his four-card suits 'upwards' until 3NT is reached or a fit established.)

Three Notrump opening and responses

This opening conventionally shows a solid minor suit and not more than a Queen outside.

(1) ♠ 7 4   ♡ 3   ◇ 9 7 3 2   ♣ A K Q J 8 6

(2) ♠ 9 7   ♡ 10 4   ◇ A K Q 7 6 4 3   ♣ Q 6

The first hand would be a minimum for the bid, the second close to a maximum.

'And what if you are doubled?' you ask.

The answer to that is that any running must be done by partner. If he does not sound Retreat, you stand fast. This is how partner should act on various types of hand:

(1) ♠ Q 10 3 2   ♡ A 8 6 4   ◇ Q J 9   ♣ 7 2

Pass whether doubled or not. The likely issue is between making or going one or two down, according to opener's strength, and Four Clubs would not be better.

(2) ♠ A 7 6 4   ♡ 5   ◇ 10 7 6   ♣ K Q 4 3 2

Whether doubled or not, jump to Five Diamonds. There should be a good chance of making it. If the hand were weaker – lacking the Ace of spades – the jump would still be right for pre-emptive reasons.

(3) ♠ A K 7 6 5   ♡ J 4   ◇ 7 6 2   ♣ 8 4 3

Take out into Four Clubs. If partner's suit is diamonds he will bid them. If opponents bid Four Hearts you will have to consider a sacrifice, but you can wait until that happens.

(4) ♠ A K 6 5   ♡ J 10 6 3   ◇ K Q   ♣ 7 5 3

Now you are likely to make 3NT, but don't redouble. You don't want to drive opponents into Four Diamonds and partner will stand the double if you do.

Other conventional responses

Some other conventional bids that can be used in response to no-trump openings are described in Chapter 13. These include the Texas convention, other transfer bids, and Three Diamonds over 2NT (Flint convention).

The traditional Acol method of dealing with big hands is by way of a strong Two bid and a forcing Two Clubs. (For a different set-up, which allows for weak Two bids in the majors, see the Benjamin convention in Chapter 13.)

The Acol Two bid

An opening bid of Two Spades, Two Hearts or Two Diamonds is forcing for one round. The most important single purpose of the Two bid is to deal with hands that cannot adequately be expressed by the sequences that follow an opening bid of One. To show what we mean by that remark, here is a hand from a standard American work on which the recommended opening is One Heart:

♠ 5   ♡ A K Q J 10 4   ◊ A 8 2   ♣ K Q 6

The thought of driving such an elephant up the narrow pathways that lead from a bid of One is alarming to an Acol player. If bids of One can be as strong as that, an excessive load is placed on such sequences as One Heart – One Spade – Three Hearts. In Acol we express such hands with a Two bid and the whole system of our approach bidding breathes more easily.

The hand quoted is a typical Acol Two bid – a hand of quality, with eight or more playing tricks. Other typical Two bids are:

(1) ♠ A K Q 5 3   ♡ A Q J 10 7   ◊ A 6   ♣ 4

(2) ♠ —   ♡ K Q J 9 7 5   ◊ A K J 10 2   ♣ 7 3

Then there is a group of hands which, as Two bids, have certain defects, but on which an opening bid of One could be worse. On these hands, where the choice lies between One or Two, there are two general tests to apply:

1. If I open with a bid of One is there any serious danger that everyone may pass and a game be missed?

2. If I open with a bid of One shall I have difficulty, after certain responses, in giving a picture of my strength?

If the answer to either question is a firm 'Yes', then a Two bid is surely right. Let us look at some examples.

♠ A J 8 7 4   ♡ A Q 5   ◇ A K 7 6 3   ♣ —

This hand lacks the playing strength of a typical Acol Two bid, but the opener would be extremely anxious if an opening bid of One Spade were followed by three passes. That is sufficient to show that it is a sound Two bid.

♠ 5   ♡ A 7   ◇ A K Q 9 8 4 3 2   ♣ Q 10

The main reason now for opening Two Diamonds is to inhibit the opposition.

♠ Q J 9 7 5 4   ♡ A K J   ◇ A K 2   ♣ 6

Some players would be unwilling to open Two on a suit that was Queen high, but this hand gives a positive reaction to both our tests. Apart from which, there is no danger in a Two bid: partner, missing two Ace-Kings, could not carry you to the skies unless he had a top spade and the Ace of clubs.

Next are two hands that do not commend themselves as Two bids:

(1)   ♠ A Q 5 3   ♡ 4   ◇ A K 7 3 2   ♣ A Q 4

This hand can be expressed by the normal processes of approach bidding: One Diamond followed by a force in spades.

(2)   ♠ 5   ♡ A Q J 9 7 4   ◇ K Q J 6 2   ♣ 3

Here you have sufficient playing values, but a Two bid is inadvisable when you are missing three Aces and the King of your principal suit.

Responding to Two bids
The response of 2NT

The weakness response is 2NT.* This should be made on all hands containing less than one honour trick and also on some stronger hands that present no attractive bid.

*See also, Herbert Responses to Two Bids in Chapter 13.

(1) ♠ K 10 8 7 4 2	♡ 10 3	◇ 7	♣ J 9 5 4
(2) ♠ J 9 8 2	♡ 7 5 4	◇ K Q 3	♣ Q 6 3
(3) ♠ K J 5	♡ 7 3 2	◇ 8 4	♣ K 10 7 4 2

Respond 2NT to Two Hearts on all three hands. The third hand does not merit a change of suit at the level of Three nor, as we shall see in a moment, does it qualify for a raise of hearts.

After a response of 2NT a simple rebid by the opener in his first suit (Two Hearts – 2NT – Three Hearts) is not forcing. Any change of suit is forcing for one round.

Opener may pass a simple preference bid, so responder should go to game on the second round whenever he has moderate values. On hands (2) and (3), for example, responder would jump to Four Hearts after Two Hearts – 2NT – Three Diamonds. On hand (1) Three Spades from responder would be forcing.

Raising the suit

An immediate raise promises at least one Ace. A double raise denotes good support but no Ace. In each of the following examples the opening bid is Two Spades.

(1) ♠ J 5 3	♡ A 8 6 3	◇ Q J 4 2	♣ 6 5

Raise to Three Spades. For this immediate raise, x x x is adequate trump support.

(2) ♠ Q 10 4	♡ 7 2	◇ K J 8 3	♣ K 7 4 2

Raise to Four Spades, showing useful values but no Ace. If partner displays slam interest you can cue-bid your Kings.

(3) ♠ Q 10 4 2	♡ 7 3	◇ K 8 6 5 3	♣ J 7

Although this hand has good distributional support there is only one second-round control and the first response should be 2NT.

Responding in a new suit

The requirement of an Ace for a positive response does not extend to changes of suit, because to insist on it there would lead to loss of time. In general, a good suit and one honour trick is sufficient for a response at the range of Two, $1\frac{1}{2}$ honour tricks at the range of Three.

♠ 7   ♡ K Q 10 7 5 3   ◇ 8 4   ♣ J 6 4 2

Respond Two Hearts to Two Diamonds, but 2NT to Two Spades.

When possible, avoid responding in a suit that lacks top cards.

♠ Q 7 6 2   ♡ A 5   ◇ J 10 7 4 3   ♣ K 6

Over Two Hearts raise to Three Hearts: do not introduce the diamonds, giving partner a wrong impression of where your controls lie.

♠ Q J 7 6   ♡ 5 4   ◇ K 7 4 2   ♣ A K 5

Now, over Two Hearts, Three Clubs is probably best.

The response of 3NT

A response of 3NT suggests a balanced hand of about 10–12 points. With trump support and an Ace it is better to raise, so 3NT conveys the inference that those values are not included; and some other bid should be found on any hand that contains two Aces.

The Acol Two Club bid

Two Clubs is opened on balanced hands that are too good for 2NT and on all hands of game-going strength that contain at least 5 honour tricks, exceptionally $4\frac{1}{2}$.

The sequence Two Clubs – Two Diamonds – 2NT suggests a balanced hand of 23 or 24 points and responder can pass on complete weakness. All other sequences are forcing to game.

Two Clubs – Two Diamonds – 3NT suggests 25 points, or at any rate a game hand in notrumps. Partner should not remove to Four of a major on a weak hand.

As between opening Two Clubs or an Acol Two, the test is whether or not you are interested in such tit-bits as partner may be able to provide.

(1) ♠ A K Q 10 7 4   ♡ A 8 4   ◇ A K 5   ♣ 6

Here you could make excellent use of ♡ K J x x x or

◊ Q 10 x x x and should open Two Clubs. If the bidding were to go Two Spades – 2NT – Four Spades you would never hear about those red suits.

(2) ♠ A   ♡ A K J 6 4   ◊ A 10   ♣ K Q 10 9 3

This time you are not interested in partner's suits unless perhaps he has good enough diamonds to mention over a Two Heart opening.

For reasons of time it is generally better to open Two Diamonds rather than Two Clubs when diamonds are the primary suit.

♠ A Q 4   ♡ A K J 8   ◊ A K 10 9 5 2   ♣ —

This is a game hand, but it may take time to find the best contract and you will save a round of bidding by opening Two Diamonds rather than Two Clubs.

A jump bid, Two Clubs – Two Diamonds – Three Hearts, sets the suit and in the first instance asks responder to name an Ace. Any subsequent cue bid by responder shows a King, or possibly a singleton with trump support.

Responding to Two Clubs

The standards required for a positive response have been steadily reduced since the early days when there was an elaborate list of qualifications like the prize list on a fruit machine. That tendency is maintained and we recommend now that when a positive response does not lose time a fair suit and a side Queen should be judged sufficient. Thus the following hands qualify for Two Hearts over Two Clubs:

(1) ♠ Q 4   ♡ K J 10 7 6   ◊ 8 5   ♣ J 6 4 2

(2) ♠ 10 7   ♡ A Q 6 3   ◊ J 7 6 4   ♣ 5 3 2

Responder should be slightly better for a Two Spade response because that call may lose bidding space when partner was intending to bid Two Hearts over Two Diamonds. Thus, on hand (1), if the spades and hearts were reversed we would advise Two Diamonds.

A response of 2NT suggests a minimum of about 8 points including two Kings, and a response of 3NT the equivalent of three

Kings and a Jack. Since these bids are space-consuming it is advisable to keep the standard fairly high.

There would be no advantage in lowering the requirements for a positive response at the range of Three, for these bids take away a round of bidding. The requirements remain at $1\frac{1}{2}$ honour tricks and a fair suit.

Responses on the second round

After Two Clubs – Two Diamonds – 2NT, responder should raise on 3 points or a five-card suit headed by the Queen. A bid of Three Clubs is conventional and is best played as Baron rather than Stayman. Opener rebids his lowest four-card suit, 3NT when his only suit is clubs. Two Clubs – Two Diamonds – 3NT – Four Clubs is also Baron.

After Two Clubs – Two Diamonds – Two Hearts or Two Spades, there are ways of indicating different grades of support for opener's suit. For example:

(1) ♠ J 10 7 5   ♡ 3   ◇ K 10 6 4   ♣ Q 6 4 2

Raise Two Spades to Four Spades. There is an inference that no Ace is held, for with an Ace and good support responder would bid Three Spades, leaving room for a possible cue bid.

(2) ♠ J 7 5 2   ♡ 3 2   ◇ K 7 4 2   ♣ 9 6 4

Raise to Three Spades.

(3) ♠ J 7 5 2   ♡ 3 2   ◇ J 7 4 2   ♣ 9 6 4

Now bid 2NT and show the spade support on the next round.

Since the requirements for a positive response at the Two level are low, it follows that when Two Diamonds has been the first response a subsequent bid in spades or hearts can be made on very little.

♠ 6 2   ♡ Q 8 6 4 3   ◇ J 6 4 2   ♣ 7 3

After Two Clubs – Two Diamonds – Two Spades it is entirely in order to show the hearts. The whole object of the present style is to enable responder to paint his picture even with the faintest of brush strokes.

Tall trees need strong roots, and good slam bidding grows from a sound basic method. Many slams can be, and should be, reached by direct extension of ordinary constructive bidding, but there are also some special techniques for the location of key cards. It is with these techniques – cue bids, advance cue bids, interest-showing bids and Four Notrump conventions – that we are most concerned in this chapter.

Cue bids

Cue bids are far more valuable in slam bidding than all the 4NT conventions put together. Acol players use them on most hands where the slam is likely to depend on special cards, and the range and application of cue bids has greatly increased in recent years.

A cue bid promises a control in a side suit. Below game level, especially, it may be only a second-round control, King or single-ton. A bid can have that meaning only when (a) a trump suit has been agreed, and (b) the partnership is by this time committed to game.

	(1)	*West*	*East*		(2)	*West*	*East*
		1 ♠	2 ♠			1 ◇	1 ♠
		3 ♣				3 ♠	4 ♣

In (1) Three Clubs is not a cue bid because, although a suit has been agreed, the bidding can be allowed to die below game.

In (2) Four Clubs is a cue bid. Suppose that as East you hold:

♠ K J 6 4 2   ♡ 7 2   ◇ A 7   ♣ A 8 5 4

Over West's Three Spades you could bid Four Spades without the Ace of diamonds, and that card you can rate as worth at least two playing tricks. You should be safe for Five Spades and there are many hands partner could have on which Six would be lay-down.

A Blackwood 4NT at this point would be a poor effort, firstly because you could have all the Aces and yet no good play for Six Spades, secondly because you could be missing an Ace and yet have a lay-down slam.

The first step should be a cue bid in the lowest suit where you can show a control. If partner accepts your slam suggestion, as by making a cue bid of Four Hearts, you can bid Six Spades without more ado. If he temporizes with Four Diamonds you can make a further control-showing bid of Five Diamonds. If partner makes the weakest bid open to him, Four Spades, you are still strong enough for a further try of Five Diamonds. Say that partner has one of these three hands:

(1) ♠ A Q 7   ♥ K Q 4   ♦ K Q J 6 3   ♣ 9 2

(2) ♠ A 10 7 5   ♥ 8   ♦ K Q 9 4 2   ♣ K 6 3

(3) ♠ A Q 10 3   ♥ J 7   ♦ K Q 10 8 5 4   ♣ 7

On hands (1) and (2) he will give you Six, but on (3) he will take note of the apparent weakness in hearts and will stop in Five.

In this example you were strong enough to persist with a second cue bid in face of a discouraging response to the first. Another time you may have to give up if your overture is not warmly received, and finally you may elicit an encouraging response but still not be able to make any further advance. Take the same auction, One Diamond – One Spade – Three Spades, and suppose that your hand is weaker:

♠ K 10 8 5 3   ♥ 7 2   ♦ K J   ♣ A 8 5 4

You have lost the Jack of spades and have the K J of diamonds in place of the Ace. Since the King of partner's suit is a most valuable card you can make one try with Four Clubs; but even if that meets with a favourable response you will have to leave any further action to partner. So the bidding may go:

West	East
1 ♦	1 ♠
3 ♠	4 ♣
4 ♦	4 ♠

With second-round control of hearts you would have bid Four Hearts over Four Diamonds. By bidding Four Spades you warn partner that you do not control the hearts.

Repeat cue bids

It is quite common for a second cue bid to be made in the same suit, by either player. Partner opens Two Spades and you hold:

♠ Q 10 6 2   ♡ A 7 6   ◇ 9   ♣ J 8 7 5 4

Holding good support and an Ace you raise to Three Spades. Partner makes a cue bid (or so you assume) of Four Diamonds and you show your Ace of hearts by bidding Four Hearts. Partner bids only Four Spades, but your singleton diamond, in conjunction with the long trumps, could easily be a decisive holding, so now you proffer Five Diamonds. You would do the same if you held the King of diamonds instead of a singleton.

Second-round controls

Kings and singletons are often the key to a successful slam, and below game level especially a player who is invited to show controls should not hesitate to do so simply because he has already expressed the value of his hand. The bidding goes:

West	East
1 ♠	2 ♡
3 ♡	4 ♣
?	

West holds:

♠ A K 7 4 2   ♡ Q 10 5   ◇ 4   ♣ Q 9 7 6

West has opened on a minimum and has raised his partner's suit. He may think he should sign off over Four Clubs, but his partner may have a strong hand and be interested in the diamond control. By bidding Four Diamonds over Four Clubs West does not say 'I am accepting your slam invitation' but 'Since you ask, I do hold second-round control of diamonds'. West is the subordinate player in this auction and it is his duty, below game level, to describe his controls.

Above game level an Ace should be named in preference to a King, but there are occasions when a player can safely mention a new suit where he has only second-round control. You hold:

♠ A K J 5 4   ♡ 9 4   ◇ J 3   ♣ K 10 8 2

Partner opens One Heart, you respond One Spade, and partner jumps to Four Spades. You have enough to suggest a slam and clearly the most helpful bid is Five Clubs. It is true that partner, if he does not hold the Ace himself, may think that you have it, but your possession of the Ace and King of trumps is protection against an excessive jump. If opener, over Five Clubs, bids Five Diamonds you can bid the slam.

In this example the cue bid of the secondary control was made by the weaker hand in the auction. That is normally the case, for the hand that makes most of the running will usually have a top control to bid. The following examples are different in that the strength is divided and sometimes the opener, sometimes the responder, cue-bids the second-round control.

(1)   *West*   *East*

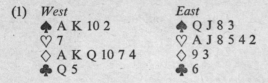

    ♠ A K 10 2   ♠ Q J 8 3
    ♡ 7   ♡ A J 8 5 4 2
    ◇ A K Q 10 7 4   ◇ 9 3
    ♣ Q 5   ♣ 6

The bidding:

West	East
2 ◇	2 ♡
2 ♠	3 ♠
4 ♠	5 ♣
6 ♠	—

(2)   *West*   *East*

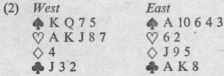

    ♣ K Q 7 5   ♠ A 10 6 4 3
    ♡ A K J 8 7   ♡ 6 2
    ◇ 4   ◇ J 9 5
    ♣ J 3 2   ♣ A K 8

The bidding:

West	East
1 ♡	1 ♠
3 ♠	4 ♣
4 ◇	5 ♣
6 ♠	——

(3)

West	East
♠ A K J 5 4 2	♠ 7
♡ Q J 7 6	♡ A K 10 9 4
◇ 7	◇ Q 8 5 4
♣ 9 2	♣ A J 10

The bidding:

West	East
1 ♠	2 ♡
3 ♡	4 ♣
4 ◇	6 ♡
——	

Advance cue bids

A common manoeuvre among good bidders is the advance cue bid, where the control is shown before the trump suit has been explicitly agreed. The usual reason is that if the suit were agreed by a direct raise there would not be an opportunity to show the control. For example, East holds:

♠ 8 7   ♡ K 10 6   ◇ K Q 8 7 5 4   ♣ A 6

The bidding goes:

West	East
1 ♡	2 ◇
3 ♡	?

A simple Four Hearts would be an underbid and Five Hearts would not be particularly helpful. East's best course is to bid Four Clubs and follow with Five Hearts on the next round.

With a slightly different holding it may be good policy to make the advance cue bid in a suit where you hold a singleton.

♠ J 6 2   ♡ K 9 8   ◇ A K 7 5 4 3   ♣ 6

Again Four Clubs would be the best bid over Three Hearts.

We noted in the chapter on notrump bidding that the notrump opener will often make an advance cue bid after such a beginning as 1NT – Three Hearts. It follows that responder will attach significance to his partner's failure to cue bid in such circumstances. For example:

West	East
♠ Q 10 4 2	♠ A K J 9 5
♡ J 10 6	♡ A K 8 2
◇ A K 7	◇ J 9
♣ Q 9 5	♣ J 3

West	East
1NT	3 ♠
4 ♠	No

By not cue-bidding over Three Spades West shows that he has a moderate opening which, despite spade support, is not especially well adapted to suit play. In the absence of such an inference East might well have essayed a slam try over Four Spades and might have been defeated in Five.

Jump to show a void

When the trump suit has been agreed, a jump in a new suit conventionally indicates a void. The bidding begins:

West	East
1 ♠	2 ◇
3 ◇	3 ♡
5 ♣	

West holds:

♠ A K J 5 2   ♡ Q 8 4 3   ◇ Q 10 7 3   ♣ —

The agreed suit is diamonds and the jump to Five Clubs, when Four Clubs would be a normal cue bid, shows the void.

Sometimes the void-showing jump will agree the suit by inference.

West	East
1 ♠	2 ♣
2 ♡	4 ◇

East holds:

♠ J 6 3   ♡ K Q 7 5   ◇ —   ♣ A J 10 8 5 2

Interest-showing bids

There is one sequence where we recommend that what would normally be interpreted as a cue bid should in fact resemble a trial bid. That is to say, the message should not be 'Rely on me' but 'Can you help me?'

The sequence is the common one beginning One Spade – Three Spades or One Heart – Three Hearts. The bid of a new suit now, Four Clubs or Four Diamonds, should be 'interest-showing'. The philosophy underlying that suggestion is that, in these two sequences, there is little value in the opener saying to partner: 'I think there is a chance of a slam and I hold the Ace of clubs.' Better that he should be able to say: 'I think there is a chance of slam but it may depend on what you have in clubs.'

This is the sort of hand where the interest-showing bid is especially useful:

♠ A K 10 5 3   ♡ A   ◇ Q J 7 3   ♣ K Q 7

After One Spade – Three Spades, neither a cue bid of Four Hearts nor a bid of 4NT is likely to resolve your dilemma. Suppose you find that partner has the Ace of clubs: a slam will still depend on whether he has second-round control of diamonds.

Playing interest-showing bids, you call Four Diamonds over Three Spades and partner directs his attention especially to his holding in that suit. Favourable holdings are K x, singleton, A x, or any stronger combination of honours. Place the following hands opposite:

(1)   ♠ Q 9 6 2   ♡ J 5 4 3   ◇ K 10 6   ♣ A 8

Responder has only a moderate raise to Three but his hand is improved by the diamond inquiry. He bids Five Clubs and goes to Six Spades if partner makes any further effort.

(2)   ♠ Q 9 6 2   ♡ K Q 5 4   ◇ 10 6   ♣ A 8 2

This is tricky inasmuch as the general strength is good and the diamond holding may or may not be bad. Opposite A x x x, for example, it is relatively good. Bid Five Clubs as before but make no further move.

(3) ♠ Q 9 6 2   ♡ K 10 9 4 3   ◇ 10 6 4   ♣ A

Good playing strength but an unfavourable diamond holding. Sign off in Four Spades.

A debatable sequence always is One Spade – Three Spades – Four Hearts. Is this last call a slam try or an alternative suit, perhaps after a prepared opening on four spades and five hearts? We recommend that it be played as interest-showing. Thus, opener holds:

♠ K Q 9 5 4   ♡ Q 7 3   ◇ A K J 6   ♣ A

Now, after One Spade – Three Spades, he bids Four Hearts.

Blackwood Four Notrumps

From the position that we accord it in this chapter, the reader will appreciate that we do not regard Blackwood as a primary move in slam bidding. The proper use of the convention is not to establish that sufficient Aces are present for a slam to be attempted, but to establish that two Aces are not missing when there are ample playing tricks for a slam. Thus the bidding goes:

West	East
1 ♠	2 ◇
2 ♡	3 ♠
4NT	

West holds:

♠ K Q 9 7 4 2   ♡ K Q J 4   ◇ 5   ♣ A J

West bids 4NT because he is entitled to assume that a slam will be playable unless partner is disappointingly short of Aces.

Another test to apply is this: *After the response to Blackwood, can you be sure where you are going?*

West holds:

♠ Q 7   ♡ A K J 6 4 2   ◇ 8 3   ♣ K J 5

and the bidding begins:

West	East
—	1 ♠
2 ♡	4 ♡
?	

A slam is likely, but to bid 4NT would be foolish because even if East were to respond Five Hearts you would not be sure whether or not there were two diamond losers. The sensible bid over Four Hearts is Five Clubs.

In the absence of special agreement, we recommend the standard responses to Blackwood: Five Clubs 0 or 4 Aces, Five Diamonds 1 Ace, Five Hearts 2 Aces, Five Spades 3 Aces; and similarly when 5NT asks for Kings. For a slightly better arrangement, see Five-Ace Blackwood in Chapter 13.

When there is intervention over 4NT

When opponents intervene over 4NT, the responder may follow the scheme known as 'Dopi'. With no Ace, double; with one Ace, pass; with two Aces, bid one step higher than the intervention (if this is considered safe); and so on.

When 4NT is not conventional

There are two obvious situations where 4NT must be regarded as a natural, quantitative bid:

(1) When no suit has been mentioned by either partner, as in such sequences as 1NT – 4NT.

(2) When no trump suit has been agreed, either directly or by inference.

West	East
1 ♠	2 ♡
3NT	4NT

Neither hearts nor spades are agreed by inference, so 4NT is natural.

Many sequences are capable of being interpreted either way, and to avoid misunderstandings it is necessary to have some prior arrangement. We recommend that 4NT in such sequences as the following should be treated as natural:

West	*East*
1NT	2 ♣
2 ◇, 2 ♡ or 2 ♠	4NT

Responder will want to use this bid in a natural sense more often than in a conventional sense. To establish a forcing sequence, responder must jump in a new suit.

In the next example a player who has made a natural bid in notrumps bids notrumps again.

West	*East*
1 ♠	2 ♣
3NT	4 ♣
4NT	

Four Clubs is forcing and East probably has a slam in mind. It is clear that 4NT from West must be reserved as a sign-off on an unsuitable hand, for he has a number of alternatives if he is interested. There are many sequences of this sort.

When a forcing bid has been made, a subsequent 4NT may be conventional though no suit has been explicitly agreed:

West	*East*
1 ♡	3 ◇
3 ♡	4NT

Here it may well be that East intends to go to slam in hearts. He has not had space in which to show support and 4NT must therefore be treated as conventional.

A kangaroo hop to 4NT is always conventional:

(1)	*West*	*East*		(2)	*West*	*East*
	1 ♡	2 ♣			1 ♡	2 ♣
	4NT				3 ♡	4NT

If the 4NT bidder has a strong all-round hand there are other ways of keeping the fire alight. The jump to 4NT is conventional and will be understood by responder to confirm the last suit mentioned.

In situations where there may be genuine doubt, follow the principle that 4NT, when not clearly conventional, is natural.

Trump asking bids

A direct 5NT, not preceded by a Blackwood 4NT, is a trump asking bid, aimed at establishing that the agreed trump suit (or a trump suit agreed by the jump) is sufficiently solid for a grand slam to be attempted.

The earliest form of this convention, the Culbertson grand slam force, which required responder to bid Seven if he held two of the three top honours, was woefully uneconomic. There are innumerable situations where a player may want to be in Seven if his partner holds just one of the top honours, or even five small.

It is possible to draw up a schedule whereby, for example, in response to 5NT, when spades is the agreed suit, Six Clubs shows no high honour, Six Diamonds one high honour, and so forth. However, this type of convention obviously doesn't work so well when the suit is of lower rank, because there is less room for expression.

Because of the great variety of sequences that may lead to a grand slam invitation, we think it better that the response to 5NT should be left to the player's judgement. A bid of the agreed trump suit is always the sign-off, signifying 'My trumps are no better than they ought to be.' Six Clubs is slightly encouraging, Six Diamonds more so, and so on. Played with this understanding, the 5NT bid can be used equally by the player who has introduced the suit, holding perhaps A Q x x x, and by the player who has raised, holding perhaps K x x x.

Baron grand slam try

When there is no room for 5NT, or when 5NT would be a Blackwood inquiry for Kings, a bid of the suit immediately below the agreed trump suit is a general grand slam invitation, saying 'Bid Seven if your trump holding is better than the minimum I can expect.'

In our previous account of the Acol system we handled 'fourth suit forcing' with delicate tongs, restricting it to special sequences and not including it in the main account of constructive bidding. The situation is different now. All good bidders follow the style whereby a bid of the fourth suit in an unopposed auction does not guarantee either length or strength in the suit named. To take the simplest example, the bidding begins:

West	East
1 ♣	1 ◇
1 ♡	1 ♠

East holds:

♠ 10 6 2   ♡ A 8 5   ◇ A Q 8 4 2   ♣ K 6

East expects to reach game but has no good natural call. It is logical, in a way, that the bid of One Spade should be exploratory, because if East had values in spades he would be bidding no-trumps.

To see how the fourth suit works, we address ourselves to these questions:

1. When should the fourth suit be bid?
2. How should you respond to the fourth suit?
3. To what level is the fourth suit forcing?

1. When should the fourth suit be bid?

There are two points to bear in mind:

(a) The fourth suit is purposeful and forward-going. Game need not be certain but it must be visible. Therefore it is wrong to bid the fourth suit just as a way of 'hanging on' in an awkward situation.

(b) The object of the call is to keep several possibilities open on hands where a limit bid would be unsatisfactory. Therefore it should be made only when there is no sound natural bid.

Let us apply these considerations to some examples:

(1) *West*　　*East*
　　　1 ♡　　　1 ♠
　　　2 ♣　　　2 ◇

East holds:

♠ A K 8 7 5　　♡ 10 7　　◇ 9 5 3　　♣ A Q 2

Game is likely but no good call presents itself over Two Clubs. If East had to choose a natural bid it would probably be Four Clubs. That would be unsatisfactory, not because the clubs are inadequate for a jump but because the bid would prejudice the chance of arriving at one of three other possible contracts.

(2) *West*　　*East*
　　　1 ♣　　　1 ◇
　　　1 ♡　　　1 ♠

East holds:

♠ 7 3　　♡ A 6　　◇ A Q 8 5 2　　♣ K J 7 3

A jump preference to Three Clubs would not be forcing, so East must temporize with a bid of the fourth suit.

Now weaken the hand so as to make it:

♠ 7 4 3　　♡ 8 6 2　　◇ A Q 8 5 2　　♣ Q 6

East still has an awkward call over One Heart, but it would be wrong to seek escape by bidding the fourth suit. East must either pass or bid Two Diamonds; with J x x of spades, 1NT would be the best choice.

Sometimes the convention (if one is to use that term) will save responder from placing too much reliance on a single suit. The bidding goes:

(3) *West*　　*East*
　　　1 ♡　　　1 ♠
　　　2 ♣　　　2 ◇

East holds:

(a)	♠ Q 9 6 5 3 2	♡ A 7	◇ J 9	♣ A 10 3
(b)	♠ A J 8 6 4 3	♡ K 2	◇ 10 5	♣ A J 5

On (a) East can see a variety of game possibilities but no adequate natural bid is available. Two Spades would not be enough; Three Spades would not be forcing and might be passed on a singleton or void.

On (b) there should be a game in Four Hearts or Four Spades or Five Clubs but it could be a mistake to hurtle at once into any of those.

(4) *West*   *East*
   1 ♡   2 ♣
   2 ◇   2 ♠

East holds:

♠ 9 2   ♡ J 3   ◇ 7 6   ♣ A K Q 7 5 4 2

Three Clubs would be inadequate, Four beyond range of 3NT. By bidding the fourth suit you exhort partner to bid notrumps if he has a hold in spades.

What to do when you actually have the fourth suit? The answer depends on the general strength of the hand.

(5) *West*   *East*
   1 ◇   1 ♠
   2 ♣   ?

East holds:

(a)	♠ A Q 9 4 2	♡ A J 7 6 3	◇ 4	♣ Q 3
(b)	♠ A J 9 4 2	♡ A K 6 3	◇ 10 4	♣ Q 3
(c)	♠ K Q 9 8 2	♡ Q 10 8 7 3	◇ 6	♣ 10 3

On (a) bid a normal Two Hearts. Partner will reply as though to a conventional fourth suit, but when you rebid hearts on the next round it will be apparent that the suit was genuine.

On (b) East could bid 3NT, but Two Hearts would be just as good. If partner has four hearts he will raise.

On a weaker two-suited hand, such as (c), one encounters a disadvantage of the fourth suit method. It is unsound to bid Two Hearts, for partner will assume that you are cheerfully disposed towards any move he may make. You have to pass Two Clubs or rebid Two Spades.

2. How should you respond to the fourth suit?

The fourth suit bidder is generally asking a question of some sort. In order of importance, he probably wants to know: Can you guard the fourth suit and bid notrumps? Failing that, can you offer delayed support for his suit? Or can you show additional length in one of your own suits?

At the same time as you answer those questions you must indicate whether or not you have reserves of strength.

(1) | West | East |
|---|---|
| 1 ♠ | 2 ♣ |
| 2 ◇ | 2 ♡ |
| ? | — |

As West you hold:

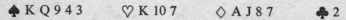

♠ K Q 9 4 3   ♡ K 10 7   ◇ A J 8 7   ♣ 2

Bid 2NT, giving priority to the guard in the fourth suit. With an additional Queen, bid 3NT.

(2) | West | East |
|---|---|
| 1 ♡ | 1 ♠ |
| 2 ◇ | 3 ♣ |
| ? | — |

♠ Q 7   ♡ A Q J 9 2   ◇ K 10 5 2   ♣ 7 6

You cannot oblige with 3NT, so the choice is between Three Hearts and Three Spades. Show the undisclosed feature of your hand, the support for partner's suit.

Make the hand slightly stronger and you still need bid only Three Spades if in doubt about the best denomination. The confidence that partner will bid again saves you from making an untimely leap.

(3) | *West* | *East* |
|---|---|
| 1 ♣ | 1 ♡ |
| 1 ♠ | 2 ◇ |

♠ A 10 9 4   ♡ J 4 3   ◇ 7   ♣ A K 8 6 2

To show heart support is the obvious move, but to what level? Never mind the minimum point count: you have three trumps and a working singleton and should bid Three Hearts. The fact that partner did not bid notrumps over One Spade means that the hands fit well.

(4) | *West* | *East* |
|---|---|
| 1 ♠ | 2 ♣ |
| 2 ◇ | 2 ♡ |
| ? | |

♠ A K J 7 4   ♡ 10 2   ◇ A 7 6 4   ♣ Q 9

On these occasions remember that partner has made a bid not less in value than 2NT and that he is looking for game. You should be the last to pour cold water on that idea, so bid Three Spades. If that is not what he wanted to hear, let him propose something different.

Holding four cards in the fourth suit, give a single raise if this can be done without going beyond 3NT. Since partner's suit may not be genuine a jump raise is never advisable; the single raise is forcing.

(5) | *West* | *East* |
|---|---|
| 1 ◇ | 1 ♡ |
| 1 ♠ | 2 ♣ |
| ? | |

West holds:

♠ A J 7 6   ♡ 4   ◇ A K 6 2   ♣ Q J 9 3

Bid Three Clubs. You are worth Four on values, but partner may be angling for 3NT. If he makes some other call you will still have a chance to show your strength and distribution.

(6) *West*   *East*
     1 ♠   2 ◇
     2 ♡   3 ♣
      ?   ———

♠ A K J 8   ♡ K Q 7 4   ◇ 5   ♣ J 10 8 2

This time you must bid 3NT, not support clubs.

3. To what level is the fourth suit forcing?

This is the sort of question on which good players dislike to be pinned down. For the avoidance of doubt, as the lawyers say, we recommend as follows:

(a) When a player bids the fourth suit at the level of One or Two, he may pass a response that depresses him.

(b) A bid of the fourth suit at the Three level is normally forcing to game.

West   *East*
1 ♡   1 ♠
2 ♣   2 ◇
2 ♡   ———

That can end it.

West   *East*
1 ♡   1 ♠
2 ◇   2NT
3 ♣   3 ♡
3 ♠   ?

East may have quite a weak hand, which indeed he has already limited with his bid of 2NT, but he must not die on his partner.

The player who has himself introduced the fourth suit at the Three level may decide to pass when his partner is clearly limited.

West   *East*
♠ Q 5   ♠ A 10 7 6 4 2
♡ A 8   ♡ 6 2
◇ K Q 10 6 3   ◇ 7
♣ A J 8 4   ♣ K 9 6 2

The bidding goes:

West	East
1 ◇	1 ♠
2 ♣	3 ♣
3 ♡	3 ♠
No	

West bids Three Hearts in the hope of nudging partner into 3NT if he holds as much as Q x x in hearts. When East can bid only Three Spades, West cannot fancy game in any department.

PART II   THE CONTESTED AUCTION

Overcalls, and defensive tactics in general, are treated quite off-handedly by players who will dispute endlessly about some trivial point in constructive bidding. Yet it is the small competitive hands that produce the swings in matches between equal teams, and doubtless that is where a lot of the points go in rubber bridge as well. We have sought to avoid the same error by devoting four chapters to contested auctions, explaining and expanding some modern ideas.

Overcalls at the level of One
(a) *Vulnerable*

Vulnerable overcalls are subject always to the tyranny of the scoring table and have not changed much over the years. The minimum standard is four more or less certain, five likely, playing tricks. The suit must be reasonable, as in a competitive situation partner will sometimes support on a doubleton. These are minimum overcalls of an opponent's One Club at game all:

(1) ♠ A 8 3   ♡ 6 2   ◇ A K 9 4 2   ♣ 8 5 4

(2) ♠ 9 4   ♡ A K J 9   ◇ K J 7 6   ♣ 8 5 2

(3) ♠ Q J 9 6 4 3   ♡ 9 2   ◇ A 8   ♣ 9 6 5

On hand (1) the playing tricks are not secure, but there is compensation in the holding of A K and A. The overcall would be slightly unsound if the opponents were not vulnerable, for then it would be a greater tragedy to lose 800 in saving the game.

Hand (2) is as weak as you dare be with only a four-card suit. Looking at this hand we have to admit that it does not conform to the 'four more or less certain tricks' standard. Many players would say that the overcall was unsound for that reason. But one has to consider these matters in the round. It is possible that your side has enough to compete at the part score level. Certainly it is better and safer to overcall now than to pass and reopen with a double over a response of, say, 1NT. That is where the 500s come from, or, equally unpleasant in their way, the 380s from 1NT doubled and made with an overtrick.

Hand (3) is short of high cards, but the playing strength is there and the fact that the suit is spades invests the overcall with pre-emptive value.

(b) Non-vulnerable

Non-vulnerable overcalls of One, like most things in life, have suffered from a degree of inflation during the past decade. The questions that used to be asked in respect of borderline overcalls were the following:

1. Is there a reasonable chance that the hand 'belongs' to your side – that you will either win the contract or obtain a penalty?

2. Is it the sort of hand on which you can envisage a profitable sacrifice?

3. Is the suit you are calling likely to present the best defence should partner be on lead?

Those are all relevant questions in their way, but there is another, less obvious, which is as important as any. That is:

4. Does the bid possess obstructive value – does it deprive the enemy of bidding space?

The simple fact is that constructive bidding is easiest to conduct when there is no interference. Even a bid at the One level has pre-emptive effect when it excludes the enemy from certain One-over-One sequences that would otherwise have been available.

Recognizing the importance of that factor, players with good competitive sense now make many overcalls that would have earned censure from the pundits a few years ago. These are some examples:

(1) ♠ A Q 7 3 ♡ 6 2 ◇ K 7 4 2 ♣ 8 5 3

Overcall either One Club or One Diamond with One Spade. It is true that you have little or no offensive prospects, also true that you could run into a fair penalty at the One level. The merit of the call is that it deprives the next player of the chance to make a One-over-One response. It may also prevent him from bidding 1NT, owing to lack of a spade guard.

(2) ♠ 5   ♡ J 9 7 4   ◇ A K J 3   ♣ 10 6 4 2

The reason why you may overcall One Club with One Diamond on this jejune assortment is a different one. In so far as you can form a judgement at this moment, the most likely game for the opponents is 3NT, for your hand has defensive possibilities against the major suits. By bidding One Diamond you may head them off notrumps. They don't know that you have only a four-card suit. Letting you into a secret, we sometimes make this kind of bid on A K x.

(3) ♠ K 10 6 4 2   ♡ 5   ◇ Q J 4 3   ♣ 7 6 2

Here, again, we would chance One Spade over One Club. Over One Heart the overcall would no longer deprive opponents of bidding space but we would still make that bid in tournament play against vulnerable opponents. That is because the scoring table favours non-vulnerable sacrifices to such a degree. Four down doubled as against a vulnerable game costs very few match points, and anything better is sheer profit.

For the same reason, a heavy penalty at the range of One is the least of the dangers attendant upon these weak overcalls. It is hard work to extract 700 from a bid at this level. In short, non-vulnerable overcalls of One are the expendable foot-soldiers of competitive warfare.

We have not qualified our commendation of these overcalls by saying 'provided partner has not passed'. Rather the opposite; as with opening pre-emptive bids third in hand, one can take more liberties with a partner who has passed than with one who may display unwelcome signs of activity.

With some rather different types of hand the fact that partner has passed makes it pointless to overcall.

♠ Q 8   ♡ Q 7 2   ◇ K J 9 5 2   ♣ A 4 2

This is not too bad a hand for constructive action, and if One Club were opened on your right it would not be wrong to come in with One Diamond. But with a partner who had passed there would be no sense in the bid. You could scarcely hope to buy the contract and by bidding you simply assist the opponents to judge the lie of the cards.

Once you decide that you have no useful part to play, there is often advantage in absenting yourself from the auction altogether. A declarer will usually misplay a hand in which the enemy strength is unexpectedly all with one opponent.

♠ A Q 8 6 4   ♡ Q 10 5   ◇ A 6   ♣ Q 6 4

After One Club on the left, One Heart on the right, there is just nothing clever in bidding One Spade, vulnerable or not. You gain no territory and you give the enemy needless information. As to the opening lead, should the hand be played on your left in no-trumps, let us hope that you will not need to send partner a registered letter to divert him from opening a diamond from J x x x x on his near-Yarborough.

Simple overcalls at the level of Two

At the range of Two the threat of a penalty double, even not vulnerable, is much greater. Apart from the fact that you are a range higher, opponents will double much more often if only through lack of a good alternative. They will also from time to time hit on the most damaging type of double – that in which the trumps are divided and the defenders can establish a cross-ruff.

Any troops that you send into battle must therefore be comparatively well armoured. Nevertheless, the tactical considerations that we noted above still have their effect.

(1) ♠ Q 6 4   ♡ 9 6   ◇ A 8   ♣ K J 9 7 5 2

This is a poor hand for an overcall at the level of Two, but not vulnerable, over an opening One Diamond, we would risk Two Clubs. We may lose 500 in a doubtful cause, but by bidding Two Clubs we obtain an advantage in space, as the chess players call it: we prevent a response of One Heart or One Spade.

Had the opening been One Spade, that advantage would no longer have existed. The only response that Two Clubs would shut out is 1NT. On balance, therefore, it would be better to pass.

(2) ♠ 9 5   ♡ Q 7 3   ◇ A K 9 6 4   ♣ A 5 2

This (in case we need to say it) is not the sort of hand on which to overcall One Spade or One Heart. You could too easily lose 300 or 500, saving nothing because you have defence to any game contract.

When both opponents are bidding, the question of whether or not to come in depends very much on the estimated lie of the cards.

(3)   ♠ 8 3   ♡ A Q 10 8 5   ◇ A 7   ♣ K 7 6 4

At love all the bidding begins: One Club on your left, One Spade on your right. To bid Two Hearts, challenging for possession of the field, would be ill-judged, for the signs are that the cards lie badly for you, correspondingly well for them. If you were doubled in Two Hearts you might well be cut up on a cross-ruff, with short spades on your left and short clubs on your right, and the King of clubs doomed from the start.

If the sequence instead were One Spade on your left, Two Clubs on your right, the prospects of a score in hearts would be much better. In fact, if you were raised to Three you could bid Four.

Responding to simple overcalls

The scheme of non-vulnerable overcalls that we have proposed will seem daring to many players, and they will need to readjust their responses accordingly. Few things are more vexing than to hazard a weak, tactical overcall and have partner crash into 2NT on values scarcely sufficient for such a response to an opening bid.

Responding on balanced hands

With a useful hand one must pause to consider: Is partner's overcall a constructive effort on which some reliance can be placed, or should it be labelled 'Fragile'?

From the analysis in the last section it will be apparent that a call such as One Heart over One Diamond must possess some constructive purpose; but One Spade over One Club may be no more than a faint cry to which one is not obliged to hearken. To be precise, one should respond to this second class of overcall in approximately the same way as to a protective bid by fourth hand: that is to say, bid 1NT on about 11 to 13, 2NT on 14 to 15.

Digressing for a moment, the same sort of discrimination should be observed in choosing a lead when opponents have contracted for 3NT. Some overcalls extend promise of a useful suit, but less reliance should be placed on overcalls (notably One Spade over a minor suit) whose object may have been to harass rather than to indicate a lead.

When partner has made an overcall that cannot be of the weakest sort, the average standard for 1NT is about 10 to 12 points not vulnerable, 9 to 11 vulnerable. However, there are no hard and fast rules. The fit with partner and the holding in the enemy suit count for more than an odd point in a side suit. For example, East holds:

♠ A 9 2   ♡ J 10 7 3   ◇ J 8 3   ♣ A J 6

With both sides vulnerable the bidding goes:

	South	West	North	East
(1)	1 ♣	1 ◇	No	?
(2)	1 ♠	2 ◇	No	?
(3)	1 ♡	2 ◇	No	?

In the first sequence you have about a maximum for 1NT.

In the second sequence you expect more from partner since he has overcalled at the level of Two. You should bid 2NT, but not more, for your spade holding is uneconomic: the four points in this suit will probably not pull their weight.

In example (3) you can bid 3NT, for here you have just the right sort of holding in the opponent's suit: only one point, but sure protection.

Raising partner's overcall

There is a difference between vulnerable and non-vulnerable raises. Vulnerable, one supports on values. That is to say, if you raise an overcall of One Spade to Two Spades, you expect to make it. In terms of general strength you assume partner to be as good as for an opening bid, with necesarily a fair suit, so that you can support on Q x or x x x.

Non-vulnerable, and particularly against vulnerable opponents, it may be good tactics to raise pre-emptively, pursuing the course that partner has initiated.

♠ J 8 7   ♡ J 5   ◇ A 9 7 3   ♣ 10 6 5 4

Left-hand opens One Club, partner bids One Spade, and right-hand passes. The opponents undoubtedly have the balance of strength and possibly a heart fit to boot, so you give a defensive raise to Two Spades. No one will have enough trumps to double and you may steal the bid or at least prevent opponents from reaching their best contract.

Changing the suit

The delicate approach bids that are common in unopposed constructive bidding have no place in a competitive auction. Changes of suit are not forcing; the new suit must, therefore, be reasonably robust. As a general principle, it is wrong to dally with a suit take-out when the values are held for a double raise.

♠ J 6 4   ♡ A 5   ♢ K 6 4   ♣ K 10 9 5 2

Here you must raise partner's vulnerable overcall of One Spade to Three, not risk being allowed to languish in Two Clubs. Nor would it advance your cause to issue a one-round force with Three Clubs: if partner went Three Spades you would still be in two minds whether or not to play for game.

The same principle applies when partner has overcalled at the level of Two.

♠ J 3   ♡ 7   ♢ A Q 10 8 6 4 2   ♣ Q 10 5

After One Spade on your left, Two Hearts by partner, you must be allowed, on occasions, to play in Three Diamonds. It is torture to hear Three Hearts (on A K J x x) and the inevitable remark, 'When you bid Three Diamonds I thought you must have the hearts with me.'

Here is the other side of the picture:

♠ 7 4   ♡ 10 3   ♢ A J 7 6 4 2   ♣ K 5 3

Now, when partner overcalls Two Hearts, the only question is whether you should pass or raise: you should not put forward Three Diamonds as an alternative contract.

A jump shift, as we said above, is forcing for only one round. The way to force to game is to bid the enemy suit; this does not guarantee any particular holding in that suit.*

*See, however, Unassuming Cue Bids in Chapter 14.

Jump overcalls

Jump overcalls – one trick higher than a simple overcall – are strong in principle but vary a good deal according to the tactical situation.

(1) ♠ A K J 7 4 2   ♡ A 8 5   ♢ 6   ♣ Q J 4

This is a standard jump overcall at any score – a strong suit and about three honour tricks.

(2) ♠ J 5   ♡ K Q 10 8 6 2   ♢ A Q 10 3   ♣ 8

Over One Club you could bid Two Hearts, not vulnerable. Two Hearts would also be a good bid over One Diamond. It might be thought that with such good defensive prospects it would be unwise to pre-empt or take any risk; but in practice this jump, with a strong holding in the enemy suit, has a way of starting opponents who have a misfit on a road to considerable ruin.

(3) ♠ K Q J 9 5 3   ♡ 6 2   ♢ K 9 7 4   ♣ 8

This hand represents a type of semi-psychic jump overcall that can freely be made when partner has passed. You have less than he is entitled to expect, but if he raises your bid the result should not be unfavourable. Vulnerable, one would prefer to have the 10 of spades instead of a low one.

Jump overcalls are best employed on one-suited hands. On two-suited hands, where a double would be unsatisfactory, a simple overcall is best.

(4) ♠ 6   ♡ A K J 9 2   ♢ 7   ♣ A Q J 8 5 2

A jump to Two Hearts over One Diamond, or to Three Clubs over One Spade, allows little space for manoeuvre. Experience has shown that the best way to keep the lines open is to overcall at the lowest level – One Heart over One Diamond, Two Clubs over One Spade. This can go wrong, but so can any other method.

Still stronger hands are expressed by an immediate overcall in the enemy suit, as described at the end of the next chapter.

Responding to a jump overcall

Partner should aim to keep the bidding open on the sort of hand that would warrant a response to an opening bid of One. Two small trumps or a singleton honour represent adequate support for even a jump raise when there are sufficient tricks outside.

A change of suit is forcing for one round.

♠ Q 5 4 2   ♡ 8   ◇ A Q 10 7 6 3   ♣ 9 2

When partner jumps to Two Hearts over an opening One Club you may try him with Three Diamonds. If he can bid no more than Three Hearts you must pass.

We have seen that in response to an overcall a bid of the enemy suit is game forcing. This is the solution to many problem hands. The bid does not show any particular holding in the suit, merely that you want to be in game and are not sure of the best denomination.

♠ Q 4   ♡ 9 6 4   ◇ K Q 2   ♣ K J 10 5 4

After One Heart on your left, Two Spades from partner, you bid Three Hearts. If partner has a heart stop such as Q x x and can bid 3NT, that will be the best spot.

Notrump overcalls

Notrump overcalls are natural in what might be called natural circumstances. If the player has passed originally, or if the bidding by the opponents is such that the overcall cannot be genuine, then the call will belong to the tribe known as the Unusual Notrump, which we describe in Chapter 14.

1NT overcall

Since it is not good tactics to overcall on moderate balanced hands, the standard for a 1NT overcall is about 15 to 17 not vulnerable, 16 to 18 vulnerable. The overcall will often contain a five-card minor suit.

♠ Q 6   ♡ K 10 6   ◇ Q 9 5   ♣ A K J 10 2

Over One Heart, 1NT is both more constructive and more

minatory than Two Clubs. If no one were looking we might make the same bid, at favourable vulnerability, over One Spade.

There are important differences between responses to an opening 1NT and responses to a 1NT overcall. The Two Club convention is abandoned, mainly because if partner were interested in a suit contract he could have made a take-out double instead of bidding 1NT.

Another difference is that there are fewer occasions when responder will want to bid Two of a suit as a sign-off. The notrump bidder, as we have seen, will often have a suit of his own and will not wish to be led down a side-turning by his partner. We recommend, therefore, that a simple take-out be constructive, though not forcing.

2NT overcall

This is generally interpreted as 'unusual'; see Chapter 14.

Protective bidding

The term 'protective bidding' is used of low-level situations where a defender has the choice whether or not to reopen after two passes. The simplest case is when an opening bid of One is passed round to the fourth player.

Since the Acol style is to join in the game when feasible and not make trap passes, it is not necessary to 'protect' on bad hands lest partner be concealing a giant. At the same time, in tournament play, where the small hands are important and no ground can be given, one has to compete when there is a fair chance that one's side may have the balance of cards.

♠ Q 10 9 5   ♡ 8 2   ◇ 9 7 5   ♣ A Q 5 4

This is a minimum for a protective One Spade when an opening One Diamond has been followed by two passes. Note that the word 'protection' is a misnomer. You do not assume that partner has a big hand (though that could be so if his main strength were in diamonds) but you are prepared to compete for the part score. The fact that you have spades improves your chances: switch the majors and it might well prove a mistake to reopen. Spades, the *corps elite* at all times, are particularly valuable in these positions, where on many hands both sides can make about eight tricks in their best suit.

On the hand above you would pass if the opening had been One Club instead of One Diamond. Two factors now enter: opponents may well be playing in a poor suit for them; and the fact that your partner has passed over One Club, though evidently not strong in that suit, means that he cannot have a good hand of any sort.

The upper limit for simple protection in a suit at the level of One is about 13 points. With more it is usual to double or, with a good suit, jump.

♠ A 7   ♡ K Q 9 8 5 3   ◇ Q 10 3   ♣ 8 4

In a protective position jump to Two Hearts over One Diamond or One Club.

1NT, especially when bid over a major suit, is one of the weaker calls that fourth hand can make. The normal standard, vulnerable or not, is about 11 to 14 points. The holding in the opponent's suit does not have to be particularly robust, for partner will often have strength in that department.

♠ J 5 2   ♡ A 9 3   ◇ A Q 8 7   ♣ 9 4 2

You are vulnerable, they are not. Left-hand opens One Spade after two passes and this comes round to you. Be bold and bid 1NT, for your vulnerable state is very likely the reason why your partner has been unable to overcall on a useful hand.

Actually, J x x is an excellent base for a protective notrump. If partner has A x x, or even K x x, you may gain by making left-hand lead. The same is true of Q x.

In pairs events players sometimes bid a protective notrump with no better than x x x in the enemy suit. They reason that (a) partner may well be at home there, with honours well placed, and (b) even if opponents run off the first four or five tricks, a good score may still be had from playing in 1NT.

On stronger hands – and some weaker ones – a take-out double is the orthodox defence. These and protective doubles are discussed in the next chapter.

In this chapter we glance only briefly at the general system of take-out doubles and responses, for in Acol these follow orthodox and well-known lines. There are, however, a number of controversial situations, many of which arise from modern competitive techniques. The chapter is sub-divided as follows:

1. Standard doubles by second hand.
2. Responses to take-out doubles.
   (a) On medium to good hands.
   (b) On bad hands.
   (c) Responding 1NT.
   (d) Responding over a raise or redouble.
3. Action by third hand over a double.
4. Doubling in the protective position.
5. Ambiguous doubles.
6. Doubles of 1NT and of a suit take-out.
7. Overcalls in the opponent's suit.

1. Standard doubles by second hand

Acol players have always steered a middle course between the very strong doublers of the scientific school and the 'shape' doublers on a mess of potage. At favourable vulnerability 10 'working' points may be just enough. For example:

♠ Q J 8 5   ♡ 7   ◇ A 10 6   ♣ K 9 6 4 2

The fact that you may be able to compete in spades justifies a double of One Heart. For a weak double, 5–4–3–1 distribution is preferable to 4–4–4–1 (not so effective in play) or 5–4–4–0 (unsatisfactory if partner passes or bids notrumps).

The following would be minimum for a vulnerable double of One Spade:

♠ 9 2   ♡ K Q 7   ◇ A J 8 7   ♣ K J 10 5

When the choice lies between a take-out double and a suit over-call, single or jump, it is worth bearing in mind that overcalls are limited and descriptive and to that extent more accurate calls than a double.

♠ J 6 4   ♡ A J 10 8 4   ◇ 7   ♣ A Q 10 6

If the spades and clubs were exchanged the preparedness for both major suits would point to a double of One Diamond. As it stands, One Heart tells the story better.

♠ K J 2   ♡ A Q 10 8 5 3   ◇ A 10 4   ♣ 9

This hand may be playable in spades, but over One Club or One Diamond the jump overcall of Two Hearts is so close to the mark that we would not forgo it in favour of a double.

The choice on very strong hands – whether to double or over-call in the opponent's suit – is discussed in section 7 of this chapter.

2. Responses to take-out doubles
(a) On medium to good hands

A jump response, such as Two Spades in response to a double of One Club, is not forcing, but the doubler should bid again unless the double was minimum and the response does not fit well.

The fact that the jump response can be passed does not mean that responder needs to give a little hop every time he is better than minimum. The test should be whether he would be worried if a simple response were passed.

♠ K 9 7 3   ♡ J 5   ◇ K 8 3   ♣ Q 7 6 2

It is not necessary to jump to Two Spades over a double at the level of One, for you will not make game if partner cannot bid over One Spade. As proof of that, if partner were to raise to Two you would not bid Four with any confidence.

♠ Q 10 6 2   ♡ 9 4 3   ◇ A K 5 2   ♣ 8 6

This is a rather borderline hand on which you might jump over a double of One Heart but not over a double of One Club. The main reason for the distinction is that it is preferable to have a doubleton in another suit than in the suit doubled, where partner also is likely to be short.

♠ J 5 3   ♡ K Q 10 9 3   ◇ A 6 5   ♣ J 7

This is about maximum for Two Hearts over a double of One Diamond or One Club. Over a double of One Spade, contradictory though it may seem, a jump to Three Hearts would hardly be adequate. The reason is that there is less room for manoeuvre at this level; the jump could be made on less than this, so it would be wise to take any strain off partner and bid Four Hearts.

A double jump signifies a long suit with moderate high-card strength: something like Q J 10 x x x and an outside King.

On game-going hands where the best denomination is in doubt the solution, as in most competitive sequences, is a bid of the enemy suit. The bidding goes:

South	West	North	East
1 ◇	Dble	No	?

Force to game with Two Diamonds on any of the following:

(1)	♠ K Q 4	♡ Q 6	◇ A 6 2	♣ Q 8 6 4 3
(2)	♠ Q 7	♡ A Q 8 7 5	◇ J 10 4	♣ A 9 2
(3)	♠ K 10 6 5	♡ A J 8 3	◇ 8 5 4	♣ K 10

On (1) your holding in diamonds is not suitable for a jump to 3NT (and you could hardly bid less on your values). If Two Diamonds produces Two Spades you can raise; if Two Hearts, your best move will be Three Diamonds; that will show the control and may elicit 3NT on K x or Q x.

On (2) Four Hearts would be precipitous. Partners sometimes have to double without the expected support in both majors. Over partner's probable spade response to Two Diamonds you can go Three Hearts and he will know what it is all about. If his next bid is 3NT the odds are that your stylish manoeuvres will be rewarded.

Hand (3) is thin for game opposite a minimum double but a force is still correct. It is the only way to be sure of the right suit.

(b) On bad hands

The system at one time employed Two Clubs as a weakness response to a take-out double. This has been abandoned – wrongly,
we believe, for the presence of a weakness response relieves the
strain on other sectors of the economy, as the politicians put it.
One of the problems of responding to a double is that responses
at the range of Two have to cover such a wide range of hands.

Although the weakness response has gone out of fashion, we
still consider Two Clubs more prudent than Two Hearts in response to a double of One Spade when you hold:

♠ 10 x x   ♡ x x x x   ◇ x x x   ♣ J x x

It is true that the doubler is likely to hold some support for
hearts, but therein lies the danger of responding in hearts: he may
raise.

With the same hand, how would you respond to a double of
One Heart? Many players would bid One Spade 'to keep it low'.
That is incredibly silly, for partner is quite likely to raise in spades.
You have a better chance to escape alive if you respond Two
Clubs. To respond to a double in a three-card major is not always
wrong, but you must have compensating values.

(c) Responding 1NT

1NT is generally regarded as a better-than-minimum response to
a double, but a distinction should be made between major and
minor suits.

♠ J 7 6   ♡ 10 8 4 3   ◇ Q J 8 6   ♣ K 10

In response to a double of One Diamond, 1NT gives the best
picture. Take away the King of clubs, and the bid is One Heart.

Over a major suit 1NT cannot always be constructive.

♠ K J 10 4   ♡ 6 3   ◇ 8 5 4 2   ♣ 7 4 2

It would be unnatural to bid anything but 1NT in response to
a double of One Spade. If the spades were Q x x x the wisest
course would be to respond Two Clubs.

(d) Responses over a raise or redouble

When third hand redoubles, responder can pass on complete weakness, or indeed on any indifferent hand that does not present a convenient bid. At the same time, a bid over the redouble by no means proclaims strength.

♠ J x x x   ♡ x   ◇ 10 x x x x   ♣ x x x

After One Spade – Double – Redouble, bid Two Diamonds rather than leave partner to step heavily on Two Hearts; but if the hearts and diamonds were reversed it would be correct to pass for the moment.

The convention known as the Responsive Double, described in Chapter 14, solves some of the problems that arise when third hand raises the opening bid.

3. Action by third hand over a double

When second-hand has made a take-out double, the opener's partner should for the most part bid naturally. With a fair hand, upwards of 10 points, which offers a chance of game or penalty, he redoubles. With a fair to moderate hand he makes a normal response, such as 1NT or a change of suit – not forcing, since the hand is limited by the failure to redouble. With a weak hand, or a moderate hand containing no feature worth showing, he passes.

2NT over a double

Most players are familiar with the convention, sometimes called the Truscott convention, whereby 2NT by third hand shows a genuine, as opposed to a pre-emptive, raise to Three of opener's suit. It follows that if the opener is better than minimum he must go to game and not bid simply Three of his suit, which would be a sign-off. This convention originally applied to the major suits, but has been extended to the minor suits as well.

A jump by third hand

The meaning of a jump over a double (One Club – Double – Two Hearts or One Spade – Double – Three Diamonds) has undergone several changes over the years. At different times it has been played as forcing for one round, as a fair hand but not forcing, and as a plain shut-out. The modern style, right or wrong, is to play it as pre-emptive – a suit such as Q J 10 8 x x and not much else. This creates a slight problem when third hand holds a hand of this type:

♠ 5   ♡ K Q 9 6 4 2   ◇ K 10 4 2   ♣ J 3

After One Club – Double, neither One Heart nor Two Hearts nor redouble is entirely satisfactory. The best practical course may be to pass and come in later.

4. Doubling in the protective position

As was noted in the last chapter, the upper limit for a simple over-call in fourth position is about 13 or 14 points. Better hands, therefore, are generally expressed by a double or a jump overcall.

Some players double only on strongish hands, from 11 points upwards, but we do not agree with that, for it rules out the obvious tactical bid on too many occasions.

♠ 6   ♡ K 10 7 5 2   ◇ Q J 8 5   ♣ K 10 6

One Spade is followed by two passes. If you are going to bid at all it is a pity if you are not allowed to double, for Two Hearts may be a blunder and it is possible also that partner would wel-come a chance to make a penalty pass of a double of One Spade.

The possibility that partner has made a trap pass is increased when the enemy suit is a minor.

♠ Q 10 7 6   ♡ K Q 4 2   ◇ 4   ♣ Q J 7 6

Opponents are vulnerable and an opening bid of One Diamond is passed round to you. You may ask, where are all the cards? Since partner has not overcalled at the range of One it is quite probable that his hand consists largely of diamonds. If so, he will be hoping that you can double.

The other side of the picture is that partner must not be too trigger-happy in passing for penalties. Since you are entitled to essay a double on attenuated values of this sort, he should be cautious on borderline hands, especially when he has a fair side suit that presents a sound alternative bid.

5. Ambiguous doubles

When advising players how to distinguish between a take-out and a penalty double, the text-books generally approve the old dictum: 'A double of One or Two in a suit is for a take-out *if made at the first opportunity of doubling* and if partner has not bid.' That proposition applies to a sequence of this sort:

South	West	North	East
1 ♣	No	1 ♠	No
2 ♣	Dble		

A penalty double.
But a delayed double may at other times be for a take-out.

South	West	North	East
1 ◇	No	2 ◇	No
No	Dble		

Here the opponents have subsided at a low level and partner is marked with fair strength. A balancing double, as the Americans call it, would be justified on:

♠ K 7 3 2   ♡ Q 9 8 5   ◇ 9 7 3   ♣ A 8

The following is a more difficult sequence to classify:

South	West	North	East
1 ◇	No	1NT	No
2 ◇	Dble		

Here the opponents again seem to be limited, but West is not in a protective position and partner still has a chance to bid. On the surface, West might hold strong diamonds. With

♠ A J 4   ♡ K 7   ◇ A Q 10 8   ♣ 7 5 4 2

he would want to double for penalties. But with

♠ Q 8 5 3 2   ♡ K 10 7 4   ◇ 4   ♣ K J 2

he might like to challenge for the part score.

The fact is that experienced tournament players seek to enjoy the best of both worlds in such situations and will double equally with either of those hands. They reckon that partner will be able to judge, from his high cards and his trump holding, which sort of double is in the air.

6. Doubles of 1NT and of a suit take-out

A double of 1NT is for penalties, even in the protective position.

South	West	North	East
1 ♠	No	1NT	No
No	Dble		

There are occasional hands where one might like to double for a take-out, but such action (on a hand not strong enough for a double on the first round) would be speculative at best. On the other hand, there are many occasions when West, in such an auction, would pass a fairly strong hand on the first round because of length in opener's suit. So, one may as well say firmly that this is a penalty double, no doubt accompanied by strength in South's suit.

To double an opening 1NT you should be at least as strong as the opening bidder. In the protective position you need to be stronger still – a fact which many players do not appreciate.

♠ K 10   ♡ K Q 10 6 2   ♢ 5 3   ♣ A Q 7 6

Sitting over a weak notrump you have a fair double; should it be passed you will have a good lead and the high cards should be well placed. But suppose you are under the bid; now it is decidedly dangerous to intervene, for you cannot rely on partner finding your suit and your hand may be quite ineffective in defence. Not vulnerable, you might contest with Two Hearts, but vulnerable that too would be dangerous. Thousands of points are lost through imprudent action at this point. Bear in mind that if opponents go two down in 1NT undoubled, plus 100 will not be a bottom for your side, but minus 180 (for 1NT doubled and made) or minus 200 (if you play the hand and go down) may very easily be.

For conventional ways of requesting a take-out after an opponent's 1NT opening, see 2NT over 1NT at the end of this chapter and also Chapter 14 (Defence to 1NT).

Responding to a double of 1NT

On balanced hands, whether weak or strong, the double should generally be left in. If you cannot beat 1NT the odds are that you will get a worse result by rescuing.

On fairly strong unbalanced hands, vulnerability and the positional factor have to be taken into account. A penalty may be inadequate compensation.

♠ Q J 10 8 5 2   ♡ 8 3   ◇ K 10 5   ♣ 7 2

You are vulnerable and the opponents not. Left-hand opens a weak notrump and partner doubles.

The best move is probably Three Spades, for it is unlikely that your long suit will play a rôle in the defence to 1NT. But if the notrump opening were on your right and partner doubled after two passes, you should stand the double because you will be on lead and there is a sure side entry for the spades.

Doubling a suit take-out of 1NT

When 1NT is doubled, third hand will often try to slip out of the net by rescuing into what may be quite a weak suit. To prevent that kind of escape, the fourth player should double freely on balanced hands containing two or more likely defensive tricks.

♠ A 8 5 3   ♡ J 8 4   ◇ 10 6 2   ♣ K J 5

After 1NT on your left, double from partner, you should double any rescue by the next player.

In these days of weak notrumps, players are well trained in evasive action and will often remove 1NT before it has been doubled.

♠ J 10 6 5 3   ♡ 9 3   ◇ 8 6 5   ♣ 10 7 4

Partner opens a weak notrump and next hand passes. Since 1NT is surely going to be doubled, responder may take the tiger by the tail and bid Two Spades, hoping that no one will have enough trumps to double this.

To counter that gambit, a double of a suit take-out in such a sequence should be regarded as primarily for business, showing strong defensive values but not necessarily accompanied by long trumps; in other words, the sort of strong balanced hand on which you would have doubled 1NT. With a good hand lacking any cards in the enemy suit, 2NT is available.

The same arrangement should be extended to doubles of a conventional Two Club take-out, for that also is frequently used by players who know that they are otherwise for the high jump in 1NT doubled.

South	West	North	East
1NT	No	2 ♣	Dble

East's double is unrelated to clubs: it indicates that he would have doubled 1NT had North passed.

7. Overcalls in the opponent's suit

The requirements for an immediate overcall in the enemy suit have been progressively lowered over the years. The overcall is no longer forcing to game: it does no more than display a powerful hand on which for one reason or another a take-out double would not be suitable.

After an opening One Diamond we recommend an overcall of Two Diamonds on each of the following:

(1) ♠ A K 10 8 4 3 2   ♡ K 4   ◇ 7   ♣ A J 6

This is not necessarily a game-going hand, but you can make the forcing overcall and then bid your spades at minimum level. Partner is not obliged to keep the bidding open to game. A jump overcall is not strong enough, and a double, apart from the danger that partner might pass for penalties, is not descriptive.

(2) ♠ A Q 10 7 4   ♡ K J 8 7 5   ◇ —   ♣ A Q 5

If partner's response to Two Diamonds is Three Clubs you can repeat the forcing overcall – Three Diamonds. That will tell him that you have the majors, and if he cannot then bid game you should pass.

(3) ♠ K Q 9 5 4   ♡ A   ◇ 9   ♣ A K J 8 3 2

Over the expected response of Two Hearts, bid Three Clubs;

not forcing, but partner will know that you have a big hand with your main strength in the black suits.

One side effect of extending the use of the forcing overcall is that, when you double instead, partner can more readily pass for penalties, knowing that you have not a freakish one- or two-suiter.

In fourth position the forcing overcall has to be made freely on distributional hands.

♠ K J 7 5 3   ♡ —   ◇ A K 10 8 3 2   ♣ Q 8

Second in hand, we would advise One Spade as the best tactical overcall of an opponent's One Heart. In the protective position Two Hearts is better than any of the alternatives. A double on this sort of hand is unwise because partner, sitting over the heart bidder, is all too likely to pass.

The forcing overcall can still be made on the giant hands. A repeat of the enemy suit will always keep the spark alive. (For a different scheme altogether, see Michaels Cue Bids in Chapter 14.)

When two suits have been bid

When both opponents have spoken, the big bid always is an over-call of the last named suit.

South	West	North	East
1 ◇	No	1 ♡	2 ♡

This is powerful, but not unconditionally forcing to game.

It follows that a bid of the suit opened on the left should be natural. That is obviously a sound arrangement in these days when One Club and One Diamond are often bid on short or non-existent suits.

Bidding 2NT over opponent's 1NT

2NT over 1NT as a forcing take-out is an old Acol bid. It is usually employed on two-suited hands where a double is likely to be a time-wasting manoeuvre.

This chapter covers, firstly, opening bids of Three or higher; secondly, the means of defence to enemy pre-emptive openings.

Three bids

'They opened *Three* at our table': so they say after many a poignant swing at match play. No one has yet devised an entirely satisfactory counter to pre-emptive bids and in the nature of things no one ever will. That is why Acol was one of the first systems to develop this form of attack.

The theory of sacrifice bidding is that it is fair to go down 500, in round figures, to save a game. On that basis a vulnerable Three opening should contain seven playing tricks, a non-vulnerable opening six playing tricks. Actually, there is more to it than that: by opening Three you may hustle opponents to an unmakable slam or to the wrong game, in which case you make a large profit. On the other hand, you will sometimes suffer a penalty when they have no game. Experienced players are more impressed by the first possibility than the second and are therefore willing to take liberties with the Rule of 500. For example:

♠ 8 5   ♡ K Q 10 9 8 5 3   ◇ 6   ♣ 10 6 4

According to the book, this is worth a Three bid if you are not vulnerable. But because the hand is virtually defenceless, and is thus especially well suited to a shut-out, you should still open Three Hearts at game all in first or third position. Second in hand, the odds do not so much favour a borderline pre-empt.

At duplicate the general keenness of play means that opponents are unwilling to take what may be an inadequate penalty. In consequence one can take greater risks in opening Three, and non-vulnerable openings on Q J 9 x x x and little else are frequently made in first and third position.

Most good players vary their game to the extent of going the other way on occasions, opening in third position especially on hands that are strong enough in high cards for a bid of One.

♠ 6 3   ♡ 10 2   ◇ A Q J 9 6 2   ♣ K Q 8

To open Three Diamonds third in hand would carry with it the risk of missing 3NT should partner have more than his share of the outstanding cards; but it is a risk worth taking, for the bid may snatch the part score or it may cause the opponents to over-reach themselves. There is, or should be, a certain poker element about Three bids. To quote from *Play Bridge with Reese*, 'A pre-empt that is known to be weak is a blunt sword.'

Responding to Three bids

To make game in a major suit opposite an opening Three bid you need about 3½ quick tricks when vulnerable, 4 when not vulnerable. When in doubt, fit the two hands together on the assumption that, not vulnerable, partner holds K Q 10 x x x x and three doubletons; vulnerable, A Q J 10 x x x and three doubletons.

♠ K Q 5   ♡ 9   ◇ A K 10 3   ♣ K J 9 8 6

After Three Hearts from partner, expect two or three losers in the side suits; more likely two than three, because a side Queen or Jack will provide extra chances. So give him Four if you are vulnerable, reckoning to lose two Aces and one other trick. Not vulnerable you should pass, but if the same strength were accompanied by two trumps you could raise with most partners.

On weak hands that contain support for partner, produce a defensive raise.

♠ J 6 5 3   ♡ 7 4   ◇ Q 8 6 4   ♣ A J 8

An advance sacrifice will generally be in order at some level or other. For example, after Three Diamonds from partner and No Bid on your right, jump to Five. If the opponents find a suit at that level you can take your chance on beating them.

In response to a Three opening, a bid in a new suit is forcing. Opener should generally raise a major suit on two or three small cards. A response in a minor will generally be a slam try.

When opponents overcall

Good judgement is especially needed when an opponent overcalls in a suit, as opposed to issuing a request for a take-out. Much of the virtue of weak Three bids is spent by premature doubles on the part of the responder. Apart from the fact that doubles based on long trumps tend to work out disappointingly, and apart also from the more obvious danger that opponents may find a safer haven, a disadvantage of doubling whenever opponents have walked into a suit of which you hold K J 10 x x is that the opening bidder cannot double any rescue bid on the strength of your call. We therefore say: double an intervening bid only when you are prepared to welcome a double by partner of any attempted escape.

Once that is agreed, the partnership can hunt as a pair. For example, you deal and hold as South:

♠ 10 6 4   ♡ 7   ◊ A J 10 7 6 5 2   ♣ J 9

The bidding goes:

South	West	North	East
3 ◊	3 ♡	Dble	3 ♠

Double Three Spades. Defensively, your hand is a good deal better than it might be.

Other pre-emptive openings

Opening bids of Four are pre-emptive, suggesting about 7 playing tricks not vulnerable, 8 tricks vulnerable. In third or fourth position Four of a major, especially hearts, may also be the best tactical bid on a strong hand.

♠ 9 2   ♡ A K Q J 7 4 3   ◊ A J 5   ♣ 7

After two passes you should worry less about a slam than about an enemy save. Put on speed with Four Hearts.

By tradition, an opening bid of Five in a major, or of Six in any suit, directs partner's attention exclusively to the Ace and King of the suit named.

♠ A K Q 10   ♡ Q J 10 9 8 5 3   ◊ A K   ♣ —

Open Five Hearts.

Defence to Three bids

As the defence to Three bids is one of the most critical departments of the game, we pause for a brief theoretical discussion.

The first point to settle is what bid to use as a request for a take-out. So far as fourth hand is concerned, the answer is easy.

South	*West*	*North*	*East*
3 ♡	No	No	Dble

East's double is for a take-out. That is plainly best because East, sitting under the opening bidder, will seldom have enough trumps for a business double. The penalties will come when West has the hearts and can pass the double. Meanwhile, all other bids by East are natural – a decided advantage.

So far all the experts are agreed, but the take-out request by second hand is a much more disputable matter. There is a choice of four popular models, as they say in the car ads: 3NT, Lower Minor, Fishbein and Double.

3NT for take-out has one pronounced weakness: 3NT over a minor suit, cutting out responses of Three Spades and Three Hearts, is a blunderbuss. (That 3NT to play is not available is relatively unimportant, for on the few occasions when one has grounds for making that call it is apt to be something of a gamble.)

The so-called Lower Minor convention, in which the cheaper minor is the request for a take-out, is used by many tournament players. However, to have to bid Four Clubs over Three Diamonds is clumsier even than bidding 3NT.

In the Fishbein convention the take-out request is a bid of the next suit: Three Diamonds over Three Clubs, Three Hearts over Three Diamonds, and so on. Both Fishbein and the Lower Minor have the advantage that a double is explicitly for penalties and 3NT to play. On the other hand, in Fishbein one of the most natural overcalls is excluded, and responder may be embarrassed when his best suit is the one called artificially.

Most players nowadays cut the knot by playing optional doubles, which are really take-out doubles, in second position just as in fourth. Then 3NT is 'to play'. In the absence of special agreement, this must be regarded as the standard method.

Whether it is the best method is another matter. One idea is to equate a double to a 15–17 notrump. The advantage is twofold: partner can judge his best action more easily than over a vague 'optional' double, and quite often the defenders will obtain their optimum result by taking a two-trick penalty. When this style is played, Three Diamonds is played for take-out over Three Clubs and 3NT for take-out over the other Three bids.

Standards for a take-out double

As a rough guide, a player in fourth position may double a Three bid on about the same values as would be required for a double at the range of One in second position.

To double at the range of Three in second position you need to be a little, but not a lot, stronger than for a double at the range of One.

♠ K 10 6 2   ♡ A Q 5 4 3   ◇ 8   ♣ K Q 2

With a Queen less you would have a double of One Diamond, so you can reasonably double Three Diamonds. It helps to maintain a standard of this kind, because partner's responses are simplified.

Overcall in the opponent's suit

An overcall in the opponent's suit is not so much a super-overcall as an indication that a pronounced two-suiter is held.

♠ K Q 10 5 4   ♡ A J 9 8 3 2   ◇ K 4   ♣ —

Over Three Clubs bid Four Clubs. Partner must not jump high on the strength of values in one suit. Suppose that he responds Four Diamonds: then you bid Four Hearts and he knows that you are long in both majors.

Defence to Four bids

At this level distinctions must be made according to the rank of the enemy suit.

Over *Four Spades* a double is for penalties and 4NT is a take-out request in all suits (not just the minors).

Over *Four Hearts* 4NT is again for take-out, with emphasis on the minor suits since Four Spades has been by-passed. A double is in principle for penalties, but there should be an understanding that a take-out into Four Spades, on a fair suit, will not be unwelcome.

(1)   ♠ A 7   ♡ A 8   ♢ K Q 7 5 2   ♣ A 7 4 2

(2)   ♠ 5   ♡ K Q 9 8   ♢ A Q 7 5 3   ♣ 8 5 2

With (1) double Four Hearts. With (2) you must pass and hope that partner can double in fourth position.

Over *Four Diamonds* or *Four Clubs* a double must be based on all-round strength, not on trump tricks. The doubler should be reasonably well prepared for a take-out into either major suit.

When sparring for a contract over an opposing pre-emptive bid, players are prone to misunderstandings over the meaning of a 4NT bid. We advise making 4NT natural except when bid immediately over 4NT of a major. For example, East–West are vulnerable and the bidding goes:

South	West	North	East
—	—	4 ♣	Dble
No	4 ♠	No	4NT

East is not at home in spades and wants to play in 4NT, holding a hand of this sort:

♠ x   ♡ A K x x   ♢ A K Q 10 x   ♣ K x x

Defence to weak Two bids

When these are encountered we recommend the same style of defence as to bids of One. Double is for a take-out, 2NT must include a guard in the enemy suit.

In Chapter 9 we advocated light non-vulnerable overcalls as a principal weapon of space war. Now we have to consider how best to manage our own constructive bidding when harassed by enemy overcalls. We study this from both sides of the table: first, as responder when second hand has overcalled; second, as opening bidder in a contested auction.

Raises and responses in competition

The old distinction between 'free raises' and 'courtesy raises' has passed into deserved oblivion, except perhaps among a few Culbertson diehards. If there is evidence of a fit with partner, the responder must take care not to be outbid. In Chapter 2 we gave this example of a sub-minimum raise of One Spade:

♠ K 7 6 3   ♡ 10 4   ◇ J 8 6 2   ♣ 9 7 4

If partner opens One Spade and there is an overcall of Two Hearts, we raise as before. The silliest thing to do is to pass and then come in with Four Spades over Four Hearts.

In the same chapter we said that K 10 x x x x and an outside Jack would be sub-minimum for a One-over-One response. When the suit is spades we make the same bid in competition.

♠ K 10 8 6 5 2   ♡ 7 2   ◇ J 9 4   ♣ 8 3

After One Club from partner, One Heart on the right, bid One Spade at any vulnerability. Make the hand a little weaker – 5–4–3–1 shape with the same high cards – and we shall still whisper (figuratively speaking) at favourable vulnerability.

We see these early rounds of a competitive auction as similar to the exchanges in a doubles match at tennis, where the side that occupies the net wins four rallies out of five. Better be up court, even though one may have to play the ball at an awkward height, than stand on the baseline making elegant passes at nothing.

Of course there are some hands where intervention makes the normal responses unnecessary or unwise. One does not bid a free 1NT on a minimum 6 points – the range is more like $7\frac{1}{2}$ to 10. Nor is there any occasion to bid weak suits on minimum hands.

♠ K 8 3   ♡ Q 9 7 2   ◇ 9 6 5 3   ♣ J 6

After One Club-One Diamond (intervention), there is no merit or purpose in One Heart. See, however, Negative Doubles in Chapter 14.

When there is a choice of responses

On moderate hands, when there is a choice between two bids, it is usually better to show support for partner.

South	West	North	East
—	1 ♣	1 ♡	?

East holds:

♠ A J 7 6   ♡ 7 5   ◇ 8 5 2   ♣ Q 10 9 3

Without interference East would bid a semi-constructive One Spade. In the present sequence Two Clubs is better for more than one reason. There is the obvious tactical point that if you bid only Two Clubs now you may be able to follow with Two Spades, whereas to bid One Spade and follow with Three Clubs would be an overstatement. Apart from that, in a competitive auction one has less time to show all the features and it is therefore important to select the most informative bid. With the guarantee of support for his main suit, partner may be able to indulge a variety of competitive fancies, including Five Clubs and 3NT.

Responding at the range of Two in a higher suit

Awkward problems can arise in any system when responder has to bid at the range of Two, if at all, and in a higher ranking suit than partner's.

South	West	North	East
—	1 ◇	2 ♣	?

East holds:

♠ K J 10 4 2   ♡ K 9   ◇ 9 3   ♣ 7 6 4 3

Is East to come in or not? A Queen more would be welcome, certainly; as things are, we make it a borderline decision.

A bid of this sort will generally be made on at least a five-card suit, but there is no rule about it. Again the bidding goes:

South	West	North	East
—	1 ◇	2 ♣	?

East holds:

♠ A 10 9 2   ♡ A 7 5   ◇ K 8 4 3   ♣ 9 3

Two Spades is safe enough, for over a raise to Three you can return to diamonds. Partner can have a weakish four-card spade suit which you will not hear about if you raise directly to Three Diamonds.

The virtue of 'space' bidding is seen in an example like this. North's Two Clubs turns a simple hand (One Spade, to be followed by a jump in diamonds) into a small problem. It was the same with the previous example.

Bidding the opponent's suit

'When in doubt, bid the opponent's suit' is a maxim that goes too far, but this is nevertheless a most useful manoeuvre on strong hands where no other call commends itself.

South	West	North	East
—	1 ♣	1 ♠	?

East holds any of the following hands:

(1)	♠ A 6	♡ A K J	◇ 9 6 5 3 2	♣ J 4 2
(2)	♠ 7 4 2	♡ K J 7 3	◇ A 10 5	♣ K Q 7
(3)	♠ K J	♡ A J 7 4	◇ A J 6	♣ 10 6 4 2

In each case an overcall of Two Spades is the best immediate action. On (1) and (2) you will be satisfied if partner can bid no-trumps. On (3) you intend to follow with 3NT unless partner makes some interesting call.

The bid of the enemy suit is still available, of course, in its old sense as support for partner's suit. At first, however, opener will cater for the sort of hand shown in examples (1) and (3).

Opener's rebid in competition

Different problems arise according to whether the enemy bidding is on the left or the right.

(a) When left-hand opponent has bid

Some special adjustments have to be made when partner has bid at the level of Two in a higher-ranking suit.

South	West	North	East
—	—	—	1 ◇
2 ♣	2 ♡	No	?

East holds:

(1) ♠ K 4 2   ♡ J 5   ◇ A 8 7 4 3   ♣ K Q 2

Here, obviously, East has no bid other than 2NT on his 13 count. Thus partner must realize that 2NT is in a sense forced and may denote a minimum hand on which opener had intended to rebid only 1NT.

(2) ♠ K 10 2   ♡ J 5   ◇ A K 9 5 3   ♣ K Q 2

The corollary to the last example is that when opener has upwards of 16 points he must look for a stronger bid that will take the strain off partner: in this case, 3NT.

South	West	North	East
—	—	—	1 ◇
1 ♠	2 ♡	No	?

East holds:

♠ J 4 2   ♡ K 3   ◇ A Q 10 5 2   ♣ A Q 9

Many players would seek escape from an awkward situation by bidding Two Spades. In this sequence, however, we think that Two Spades should confirm support for partner's hearts. If that is the understanding, the best that East can do is bid Three Clubs.

He may well have a chance on the next round to bid Three Spades, inviting 3NT.

(b) When right-hand opponent has bid

The opener is now relieved of the obligation to rebid, so we have another 'free bid' situation. On moderate hands the question is not so much 'Have I anything in reserve?' as 'Have I anything useful to contribute?'

South	West	North	East
—	—	—	1 ♡
No	1 ♠	2 ♣	?

East holds:

(1)	♠ Q 5	♡ A Q 7 6 3	◊ A J 10 3	♣ 9 2
(2)	♠ J 9 6	♡ A Q 10 3	◊ Q 7 5 4	♣ A 8
(3)	♠ J 5	♡ A J 10 6 5 3	◊ A 7 3	♣ 8 5

These are all close to minimum openings but in each case East should make the natural call – Two Diamonds, Two Spades, and Two Hearts respectively.

South	West	North	East
—	—	—	1 ♠
No	2 ♣	2 ♡	?

Both sides are vulnerable and East holds:

♠ A Q 7 6 4   ♡ Q 4   ◊ K Q 9 8   ♣ Q 3

Here, by contrast, you have quite a strong opening, but in a tactical sense nothing is gained by bidding over Two Hearts. Rather, you want to hear what partner will say next.

A 'reverse' in competition

Misunderstandings often occur when the opener is obliged to bid his second suit at a higher level than would have been necessary had there been no intervention. Compare these two sequences:

(1)	South	West	North	East
	—	—	—	1 ♡
	No	2 ♣	2 ◊	2 ♠

A normal reverse; North's bid has not raised the level of the auction for East.

(2)

South	West	North	East
			1 ♣
1 ◇	1 ♡	2 ◇	2 ♠

'You reversed!' says West later, having carried the partnership too high. But his ear has deceived him. East was planning a simple sequence: One Club – One Heart – One Spade. The intervention forced him to go higher; he will not be minimum but there is no justification for placing him with reversing values.

When partner has redoubled

A player who redoubles pledges himself to make one further call if the bidding comes round to him again at a low level. Thus a convention has grown that opener is expected to pass on any fair hand; if he bids in front of the redoubler he is strictly limited. The bidding goes:

South	West	North	East
	No	No	1 ♠
Dble	Rdble	2 ♣	?

East holds:

(1)   ♠ K Q 10 7 4 3   ♡ 6 2   ◇ K 8 7   ♣ 10 3

East must bid Two Spades at once, to warn partner that he is not up to strength.

(2)   ♠ A K 8 6 4   ♡ J 5   ◇ A Q 6 2   ♣ 10 3

East must pass. Two Diamonds would be a mistake (a) because it would suggest a rather weak two-suiter and (b) because partner may be intending to double Two Clubs.

(3)   ♠ K Q J 8 6   ♡ K 9   ◇ A 6 3 2   ♣ 9 5

East must pass on this round and bid Two Spades if partner doubles Two Clubs or bids Two Hearts.

The same sort of considerations apply if North passes the redouble. On (1) East must bid Two Spades immediately.

Penalty doubles at low levels

Neither in this chapter nor the one before have we said much about penalty doubles, for these are mostly a matter of judgement rather than system. It is, however, advisable to have an understanding about the co-operative quality of low-level doubles; that is to say, to what extent should the opener use his judgement in accepting or rescuing the double of a part-score contract?

A double of *Three Diamonds* or *Two Hearts*, which would give the opponents game if it were made, should be solidly based on defensive tricks. Opener should seldom rescue unless he is void of the suit doubled. At game all the bidding goes:

South	*West*	*North*	*East*
—	—	No	1 ♣
2 ♡	Dble	No	?

East holds:

(1) ♠ K Q 9 6 3 2   ♡ 5   ◇ A Q 8   ♣ 10 7 4

He has a minimum opening, certainly, but he has his quota of defensive tricks and is not called upon to rescue.

(2) ♠ K Q 9 6 3   ♡ —   ◇ Q J 9 5 2   ♣ A 7 4

Now it is advisable to remove the double for two reasons: your void in hearts may prove a serious disadvantage, and you have a second suit. Partner's double may include ◇ A K x x and his expected tricks in this suit will not materialize in the defence against hearts. East should take out into Three Diamonds rather than Two Spades, for the doubler is likely to be short in spades.

(3) ♠ K J 7 4 2   ♡ —   ◇ A 10 7 4   ♣ K 9 6 3

Now East may regret that he opened the bidding, but he has nowhere to go over Two Hearts doubled and must hope to beat it.

A double of *Two Diamonds* or *Two Clubs* is a different matter, for it is often the best action on quite moderate trumps, no better than K x x. Opener should treat these doubles as co-operative and, though he may occasionally miss a ripe plum, should take out on any unsuitable hand. Thus, reverse the red suits in example (1) above:

♠ K Q 9 6 3 2   ♡ A Q 8   ◇ 5   ♣ 10 7 4

Having opened One Spade, East should not hesitate to take out a double of Two Diamonds.

A penalty double of *One Heart* or *One Spade* can be played in two ways: as heavy stuff, based on powerful trumps, or as highly co-operative, with perhaps not more than K 9 x x of the enemy suit. These cream-puff doubles are not part of the Acol style. We think the best use of a double at the One level, especially when vulnerable, is to indicate a powerful holding in the opponent's suit, but little else.

At game to East–West the bidding goes:

South	West	North	East
—	1 ◇	1 ♠	?

East holds:

(1) ♠ K Q 10 9 3   ♡ 7 5   ◇ 7 2   ♣ Q 6 4 2

This hand is right for the double; there may be nothing better for your side.

(2) ♠ A J 9 3   ♡ K J 5   ◇ 7 2   ♣ J 9 8 4

Now refrain from doubling. We think the hand well worth 2NT, but if you don't like that, bid Two Clubs.

Players normally double *1NT* whenever it is apparent that their side holds the balance of the cards. There are certain hazards in this, particularly in tournament play. Resourceful defenders, at favourable vulnerability, may lay their heads on the block and invite the executioner to do his worst. If they play in a psychic 1NT doubled and suffer the axe to the extent of six down, they have registered a substantial gain as against a vulnerable slam.

Because of this, we have suggested in the previous version of Acol and elsewhere that the vulnerable side should double 1NT only when it looks as though the bid is genuine and the best result may be to take a small penalty. Thus, after One Heart – 1NT, we recommend a double on 8 to 10 points, but not on any stronger hand. A bid of a new suit at the Two level should be treated as forcing, as though there had been no intervention. This advice, admittedly, has not made much impact on the ingrained habits of rubber bridge players, so we put it forward, not as part of the Acol system, but as an idea worth bearing in mind, especially against opponents who are prone to intervene with a 'comic notrump'.

PART III　TOURNAMENT ACOL

The first two parts of this book have presented the factory model of the Acol system. The last two chapters are the racing model. One difference is that in the earlier part, while we may have mentioned alternative treatments, we have always made a positive recommendation, so that a pair that has agreed to play Acol in the style of this book will have a common point of reference; in this later part we present optional extras, some of which can be played in different ways and a few of which are exclusive of one another. Thus a pair that proposes to play tournament Acol will need to agree on the conventions, or styles, described in these two chapters. Dealing first with areas of constructive bidding, we list the following:

1. Herbert responses to Two bids
2. Benjamin Two bids
3. Swiss convention
4. Delayed game raise
5. Five-Ace Blackwood
6. Texas Four Clubs and Four Diamonds
7. Weak notrump throughout
8. Transfers over 1NT
9. Flint convention over 2NT
10. Transfers over 2NT
11. Crowhurst convention

1. Herbert responses to Two bids

The Acol machinery for big hands, both Two Clubs and the other Two bids, is not the best part of the system; the modern One Club systems have an advantage in this area. However, the Acol method can be improved to a surprising extent by playing Herbert responses to Two bids. The Herbert convention was devised originally for the responses to a take-out double: a bid of the next suit was a weakness response. Thus Herbert over a Two bid means that the weakness response is not 2NT but the next suit – Two Hearts over Two Diamonds, Three Clubs over Two Spades.

When responder wants to give a positive in the 'Herbert' suit he saves space by bidding 2NT. South opens Two Hearts and North holds:

♠ A Q 8 5 2　　　♡ 7　　　♢ K 9 5 2　　　♣ 7 4 3

The response to show a positive in spades is 2NT.

Herbert responses save a round of bidding in many sequences and are particularly useful on a type of hand that tends to be bad for Acol:

♠ J x　　　♡ A K Q 10 x x　　　♢ A K x　　　♣ K x

Whatever you open can be a grisly error. The usual solution is to open Two Hearts and raise 2NT to 3NT, hoping for the best. Playing Herbert responses, you open Two Hearts, partner gives you a negative of Two Spades, and now you bid 2NT. A notrump contract is played from your side and if partner has nothing he can pass 2NT.

2. Benjamin Two bids

This is an ingenious scheme that enables Acol players to incorporate weak Two bids in the major suits.

All Acol Two bids are opened Two Clubs. The weakness response is Two Diamonds, and opener's rebid is not forcing. The sequence Two Clubs – Two Diamonds – 2NT can be played as 21–22, slightly stronger than an opening 2NT. It is possible to make the equivalent of our Acol Two bid in clubs by following the sequence Two Clubs – Two Diamonds – Three Clubs.

With a normal Two Club hand the opener bids Two Diamonds, to which the weakness response is Two Hearts. Responder with a positive in hearts may have to bid Three Hearts over Two Diamonds, as it is desirable to retain 2NT to show scattered values. After Two Diamonds – Two Hearts, opener bids in the same style as after an orthodox Two Clubs – Two Diamonds.

The Benjamin method does not add much to the bidding of strong hands, but it has the important advantage of freeing Two

Hearts and Two Spades for use as weak Two bids – about 7–11 with a six-card suit. Over a weak Two bid the only forcing response is 2NT. A raise to Three of the major suit is not a game try. Over the 2NT response opener who is minimum rebids his suit at the Three level; any other rebid indicates a feature. Say that you open Two Spades, as dealer at love all, on:

♠ A Q 10 8 4 2   ♡ 4   ◇ K J 2   ♣ 7 4 3

Over 2NT you bid Three Diamonds.

One consequence of using weak Two bids is that more reliance can be placed on the defensive quality of opening One bids. The bids of Two Hearts and Two Spades should be treated as an integral part of the system, not as puny weapons for felonious assault.

3. Swiss convention

After an opening One Heart or One Spade, responses of Four Clubs and Four Diamonds are comparatively idle. They have therefore been enlisted to portray certain classes of game raise, somewhere between a sound raise and a force. Over One Heart you hold:

♠ K 5   ♡ A J 7 4   ◇ K J 6 3   ♣ Q 8 4

This is strong for One Heart – Four Hearts and below standard for a force. Playing the Swiss convention you respond, depending on your method, either Four Clubs or Four Diamonds.

There is no general agreement about the exact use of these two responses. Some partnerships bid Four Clubs only with a specific holding such as two Aces and a singleton. Some just say that Four Clubs should be more of a slam suggestion than Four Diamonds (the logical arrangement because there is room for partner to indicate general acceptance by bidding Four Diamonds over Four Clubs). Some say that these responses should not contain a singleton, since a different approach is possible on shapely hands. Some hold that Four Diamonds should stress the quality of the trump support – K Q x x or better. There is much to be said for combining these last two requirements: use Swiss on comparatively balanced hands in the 12–15 range, bidding Four Diamonds when the trump support is particularly strong.

Extended Swiss can be used in a sequence such as One Diamond – One Heart – Four Clubs. Here Four Clubs would be a raise to game on a fairly balanced hand.

4. Delayed game raise

Two long suits, a fit, and sufficient controls will sometimes produce an easy twelve tricks even when the combined point count is in the middle twenties.

West	East
♠ A Q x x x	♠ K J x x
♡ x	♡ x x x
♢ A 10 x x	♢ x
♣ K x x	♣ A Q J x x

Only 24 points, but a lay-down slam. The method known as 'delayed game raise' makes it quite easy to bid. Over One Spade East bids Two Clubs, West Two Diamonds, and East Four Spades. The sequence promises good trump support and a fair side suit. West presses on with Five Clubs, East shows his control in diamonds with Five Diamonds, and West can then bid the slam.

Sometimes a player who intends to give a delayed game raise will apparently be frustrated by his partner's rebid. The bidding goes:

West	East
1 ♡	2 ♢
2 ♡	4 ♣

East bids Two Diamonds, intending to follow with a delayed game raise. However, to jump to Four Hearts over the rebid of Two Hearts would be a normal raise. If East thinks there may be a chance of a slam, he jumps in the other minor suit.

A sequence such as One Spade – Two Clubs – 2NT – Four Spades denotes DGR values, because Three Spades over 2NT would be forcing.

5. Five-Ace Blackwood

A variation in the responses to Blackwood will make a difference on occasions. When the responder to 4NT holds two Aces he responds as follows:

With 0 or 3 Aces, Five Clubs.

With 1 or 4 Aces, Five Diamonds.

With 2 Aces and no King of a genuine suit bid by the partnership, Five Hearts.

With 2 Aces and one such King, Five Spades.

With 2 Aces and two such Kings, 5NT.

This method of responding with two Aces is perhaps more useful in a negative than in a positive sense. For example:

West	East
♠ K Q 10 7 4 2	♠ A 8 3
♡ Q 5	♡ K 6
◇ A J 4	◇ K Q 3
♣ Q 6	♣ A 10 7 4 2

The bidding goes:

West	East
1 ♠	3 ♣
3 ♠	4 ♠
4NT	5 ♡
5 ♠	No

The response of Five Hearts tells West that an Ace is missing and also the King of clubs.

Here is an example of a favourable reply:

West	East
♠ K Q 10 4	♠ A J 9 2
♡ A 8	♡ K 10 5 3
◇ A Q J 6 4	◇ K 5
♣ 8 7	♣ A 4 2

The bidding goes:

West	East
1 ◇	1 ♡
1 ♠	4 ♣ (extended Swiss)
4NT	5NT
7 ♠	No

6. Texas Four Clubs and Four Diamonds

These transfer openings have been around for a long while now. They serve for hands that are too strong for a pre-emptive opening of Four of a major but lack the quality for an Acol Two bid. Four Clubs denotes a heart suit, Four Diamonds a spade suit. These are typical hands for the convention:

(1)   ♠ 6   ♡ A Q J 9 7 5 2   ◇ K Q J 4   ♣ 3

(2)   ♠ A K J 10 8 5 3   ♡ A 7 4   ◇ 4   ♣ 6 2

On (1) open Four Clubs. If partner sees slam possibilities he will make a bid of the intermediate suit, Four Diamonds (this having no relation to diamonds). Opener in this case will not accept the first slam invitation. With the second hand, obviously, he will; after Four Diamonds – Four Hearts he will cue-bid his Ace of hearts.

7. Weak Notrump throughout

Without going into a theoretical discussion, we will record that a majority of tournament players use a weak notrump whether vulnerable or not. At pairs, especially, the threat of a possible 800 is less intimidating than at rubber bridge or even at IMP (international match points). Meanwhile, you are able to play a lot of hands in the 'good' contract of 1NT, and quite often opponents will fall into a trap by competing. There is also the advantage of a uniform style irrespective of vulnerability.

8. Transfers over 1NT

The first form of Texas response to 1NT was Four Diamonds to request a transfer to Four Hearts, Four Hearts to request a transfer to Four Spades. As the second of these was highly accident-prone, players adopted 'South African Texas', whereby Four Clubs asks for Four Hearts, Four Diamonds for Four Spades. This is an improvement on ordinary methods, but most players have adopted transfers at the Two level. The scheme is:

Two Clubs remains a Stayman inquiry.
Two Diamonds is a transfer to Two Hearts.
Two Hearts is a transfer to Two Spades.

Two Spades signifies a raise to 2NT.

2NT is a transfer to Three Clubs. If responder is weak, with clubs, he will pass; if he is weak, with diamonds, he will transfer to Three Diamonds. (Further developments are possible. For example, after 1NT – 2NT – Three Clubs, responder may bid Three Hearts or Three Spades to denote a singleton in the suit named, 3NT to denote a good minor two-suiter).

Three Clubs and *Three Diamonds* are not forcing; they signify a long, broken minor suit and invite opener to bid 3NT only if he has a good fit for the minor, K x x or better.

Three Hearts and *Three Spades* are invitational and show a good suit, such as Q J 10 x x x, playable opposite a doubleton.

Four Clubs is Gerber, asking for Aces.

Opener's rebids after the transfer responses of Two Diamonds or Two Hearts

Opener is not obliged to bid simply Two Hearts over Two Diamonds, or Two Spades over Two Hearts. If close to maximum for his 1NT (whether weak or strong), and with a good three-card holding in partner's major, he may rebid 2NT. With four-card support for partner's major and a promising hand for game, he may jump to Three of the major or introduce another suit at the Three level in which he holds values.

To lessen the likelihood of going overboard when responder is weak and does not wish to play above the Two level, some variations are introduced into sequences following a Stayman Two Club response. Briefly, Two Spades, following Stayman, is always a sign-off; so is Two Hearts, in the sequence 1NT – Two Clubs – Two Diamonds – Two Hearts. A responder who is weak, with five spades, can always begin with Two Clubs; a responder who is weak, with hearts, will not be able to begin with Two Clubs when he cannot stand a Two Spade call by the opener.

(1)   ♠ J 6 3   ♡ Q 10 7 4 2   ◇ 5   ♣ 8 4 3 2

(2)   ♠ 7 4   ♡ J 9 7 5 3   ◇ Q 8 5 2   ♣ 6 4

With (1) responder can bid Two Clubs over 1NT because a rebid of Two Spades by opener will not embarrass him. On (2) he must either pass or respond with a transfer of Two Diamonds, taking the risk that opener may bid an inconvenient 2NT. We advise a pass until doubled.

Continuations by responder after a transfer bid

One of the big advantages of transfers is that responder can express a balanced hand containing a five-card major. A sequence such as 1NT – Two Hearts – Two Spades – 2NT or 3NT will indicate probably a 5–3–3–2 type with sufficient for the raise. Opener will play in the suit or in notrumps, depending on support and texture.

A new suit by responder, following a transfer, is forcing for one round and presumptively shows a second suit. Responder is in charge, however, and may be just testing the opener's reaction.

A sequence such as 1NT – Two Hearts – Two Spades – Three Spades indicates a six-card suit and is generally played as forcing; opener is invited to name controls.

The Baron sequence

A special significance attaches to the sequence 1NT – Two Diamonds – Two Hearts – Two Spades. This is not needed to portray a major two-suiter and initiates instead a Baron-type inquiry for four-card suits, which are bid 'upwards' until 3NT is reached or a fit is discovered. The method is employed mostly on good 4–4–4–1, 4–4–3–2 or 5–4–3–1 responding hands and is particularly useful in discovering a 4–4 fit in a minor suit. Sometimes partner's rebid over Two Diamonds will temporarily frustrate the responder's intentions. For example, the bidding may begin 1NT – Two Diamonds – 2NT. Now responder, who was proposing to follow Two Hearts with Two Spades, must bid spades at the Three level to restore the Baron inquiry.

The effect on other sequences

We have noted that a direct jump to the Three level is not forcing when transfers are played. On the other hand, any new suit at the Three level, following Stayman, is forcing. Thus a strong hand with a long minor suit can be launched by way of 1NT – Two Clubs – Two any – Three Clubs (or Three Diamonds). This is in accordance with what is called the Principle of Fast Arrival. When a player by-passes a conventional sequence and gives a direct response, such as Three Hearts over 1NT, he is weaker than if he had employed a conventional Two Clubs on the way.

The South African Texas responses of Four Clubs and Four Diamonds are clearly not required when transfers are played. A simple idea is to play these as a raise to 4NT with a five-card minor. Jumps to Four Hearts or Four Spades are 'to play'.

Summary of the transfer method

We have said enough to indicate that transfers over 1NT greatly increase the range of expression. They contain almost no disadvantage and are one of the first areas of bidding that a new partnership should study.

9. Flint convention over 2NT

This was one of the first essays in transfer bidding. The object is to enable the partner of a 2NT opener who has a weak hand with a long major suit to play at the Three level.

Over 2NT the responder bids Three Diamonds, requesting opener to rebid Three Hearts. If responder has a weak hand with hearts, he passes. If he has a weak hand with spades he bids Three Spades, and opener is expected to pass this.

The 2NT opener will sometimes be willing to take a chance on game opposite any hand that contains the right six-card suit.

West	East
♠ A 10	♠ 7 4 3
♡ A 8 5 3	♡ J 9 7 6 4 2
◇ K Q J 4	◇ 6
♣ A K 5	♣ 9 4 2

West opens 2NT and East responds Three Diamonds, aspiring to settle in Three Hearts. West, however, is prepared to play in game opposite any hand with long hearts. He rebids Three Spades, allowing partner to subside in spades, should this be his suit, or go to Four Hearts.

Occasionally, the 2NT opener may be strong enough to fancy game whether partner has spades or hearts. In this case he rebids 3NT.

The Flint convention does not exclude the use of Three Diamonds in its natural sense. A sequence such as 2NT – Three Diamonds – Three Hearts – 3NT annuls the first meaning of the response and shows a hand with slam possibilities containing a diamond suit.

10. Transfers over 2NT

Transfers over 2NT confer an advantage, just as over 1NT. The scheme is:

Over 2NT, *Three Clubs* is Stayman inquiry, although (as mentioned in Chapter 5) some players prefer to play it as Baron.

Three Diamonds is a transfer to Three Hearts. Responder with a weak hand may pass this, obtaining the same result as when using the Flint convention.

Three Hearts is a transfer to Three Spades.

Three Spades denotes interest in at least one minor suit and expresses doubt about 3NT. Opener who has both majors well guarded and is not particularly suitable for slam in a minor may rebid 3NT. If not well upholstered in the majors he can bid Four Clubs, to discover responder's intentions. (Other conventional bids are available, such as Four Hearts to show good support for clubs, Four Diamonds to show preference for diamonds, 4NT to indicate good values in both minors.)

Over the transfer bids of Three Diamonds and Three Hearts, opener who is particularly strong may rebid 3NT (with a holding of not less than A K x in partner's suit) or go to game in the indicated suit or cue-bid at the Four level.

Transfers have the advantage of making the strong hand declarer and often lead to a gain in space. A simple example is 2NT – Three Hearts – Three Spades – 3NT, where responder shows a fairly balanced hand which includes five spades. In a sequence such as 2NT – Three Diamonds – Three Hearts – Four Diamonds responder expresses a two-suiter more economically than would be possible if the bidding had begun 2NT – Three Hearts – Four Hearts.

11. Crowhurst convention

After a rebid of 1NT, in a sequence such as One Diamond – One Spade – 1NT, Two Clubs by responder is a conventional inquiry for range and distribution. It has this meaning even when the opening bid was One Club.

The convention has two important advantages: it enables responder to rebid 1NT on a much wider range than usual – 12 to 16 – and it leads to more accurate expression after the rebid.

The convention has passed through many theoretical stages. We recommend the version in which, after One Diamond – One Heart – 1NT – Two Clubs, opener rebids as follows:

With a minimum 12–13, *Two Diamonds*.

With a medium 14–15 and three cards in partner's suit, *Two Hearts* (partner having called hearts).

With a medium 14–15 but only a doubleton or singleton in partner's suit, Two of the 'other major', in this case *Two Spades*.

With a maximum 16, *2NT* (or possibly a jump to the Three level in responder's suit).

The sequence One Club – One Diamond – 1NT is also 12–16 and Two Clubs by responder is conventional. Opener with a medium 14–15 will bid the major in which he holds better values.

Second-round bids by responder which by-pass the Crowhurst Two Clubs are mostly non-forcing, in accordance with the Principle of Fast Arrival (see section 8 above). After the same sequence, One Diamond – One Heart – 1NT, non-Crowhurst bids would have the following meaning:

Two Diamonds, rather weak, with support for diamonds.

Two Hearts, a sign-off.

Two Spades, forcing for one round but probably just a distributional hand.

2NT, natural raise, 10–11.

Three Clubs, a limited hand with four hearts and six clubs, not good enough for a first-round response of Two Clubs.

Three Diamonds, good distributional support, but limited.

Three Hearts, invitational, with a good suit, but not forcing.

It follows that bids at the Three level, when a Crowhurst Two Clubs has preceded, are forcing.

It is surprising, really, how slow the bridge public is to adopt new bidding styles of undoubted merit. A convention such as the negative double has been around for nearly thirty years but is used only by tournament players. Of the conventions listed below, the Unusual Notrump is the only one that has percolated among club players, let alone private-house players, and they make the worst of it!

1. Unusual notrump
2. Responsive doubles
3. Extension of rescue redoubles
4. When a cue-bid is doubled
5. Michaels cue-bids
6. Defence to 1NT
7. Competitive doubles
8. Unassuming cue-bids
9. Negative doubles

1. Unusual Notrump

This convention is well known, but there are one or two points that need to be clarified.

In general, when an overcall in notrumps cannot be genuine it is classified as 'unusual' and signifies distributional values in the lowest unbid suits. These are some sequences where a doubt may possibly exist:

South	West	North	East
1 ♡	2NT		

Though the overcall could logically be genuine, it is treated as unusual.

South	West	North	East
1 ♥	No	No	2NT

Here East quite possibly has a good minor suit, but his 2NT is natural. With a minor two-suiter he must begin with Two Diamonds or Three Diamonds.

South	West	North	East
No	1 ♣	No	1 ♥
1NT			

South's 1NT cannot be genuine after his original pass. A second-round double would also denote values in the unbid suits, but 1NT indicates a more shapely hand, with fewer tricks.

South	West	North	East
1 ♠	No	2 ♥	2NT

Unusual, because it is most unlikely that East would have the values for a natural 2NT after an opening bid and a response at the range of Two.

South	West	North	East
1 ♥	2 ♣	2 ♥	No
No	2NT		

As West bid simply Two Clubs over One Heart he cannot be bidding 2NT in a natural sense. Here the bid suggests a hand with both minor suits, but the clubs are obviously longer than the diamonds. West is saying that he wants to compete in clubs or diamonds.

A point to bear in mind about the unusual notrump is that if opponents eventually buy the contract the declarer will have a valuable guide to the distribution of the unseen hands. It is therefore unwise to brandish this toy except when you have a definite possibility of challenging for the contract. At game to North-South the bidding begins:

South	West	North	East
1 ♥	No	1 ♠	?

East holds:

♠ 6   ♥ 5 2   ◇ K J 8 6 3   ♣ A 8 6 4 2

It is absurd to come in with 2NT (or, indeed, to overcall an opening bid with 2NT on these values). By so doing you offer opponents an easy option. If they have a misfit they will play for a penalty, and if instead they win the contract either in a suit or notrumps they will benefit considerably from the knowledge that one defender holds ten cards in the minor suits.

2. Responsive doubles

Responsive doubles occur when there has been a take-out double and the opener's partner has raised, as in this sequence:

South	West	North	East
1 ♠	Dble	2 ♠	Dble

East's double is, as it were, a 'return' double: he has values but no good call to make at the Three level.

If North had changed the suit over West's double, then the double by East would of course have been for penalties. (We mention this point because we have recently seen a book where the function of a responsive double was misrepresented.)

A double up to Three Diamonds (in the sequence One Diamond – Double – Three Diamonds) is responsive by definition. A double of Three Hearts or Three Spades might be described as cooperative; it should not be based on trump tricks alone.

3. Extension of rescue redoubles

Whenever a part-score contract has been doubled for penalties – or there has been a penalty pass of a take-out double – a redouble is SOS. It is logical to assume that a player who has been doubled in a part-score and who is satisfied with the contract, will pass.

South	West	North	East
1 ♡	2 ♣	Dble	Redble

East's redouble is a rescue attempt. The enemy suit is a possible landing-place in such an emergency.

The Kock-Werner redouble (of which this is an example) used to apply to suit contracts at the level of One or Two. It is extended nowadays to notrump contracts and may even occur at the Three level in a sequence such as:

South	West	North	East
1 ♠	2 ◇	3 ♣	Dble
Redble			

South, who holds

♠ K Q 9 8 5 3   ♡ A 10 6 4   ◇ Q 9 2   ♣ —

cannot fancy Three Clubs doubled and if he decides to redouble it will be for a rescue.

4. When a cue-bid is doubled

The bidding goes:

South	West	North	East
1 ♠	No	2 ♡	No
4 ♡	No	5 ♣	Dble
?			

After North's cue-bid has been doubled, South should have a method of indicating his holding in the suit. The Italian scheme, which seems as good as any, is:

With first-round control (of clubs), redouble.

With second-round control (King or singleton), pass.

With two or more losers, bid something.

In the present sequence, Five Diamonds by South would imply two losers in clubs and probably Ace of diamonds.

5. Michaels cue-bids

To play the overcall in an opponent's suit, Two Hearts over One Heart, as a giant take-out double makes very poor use of a simple call, even if the giant is reduced in stature, as suggested in Chapter 10. The Michaels cue-bids give this call much more employment, in the way of an aggressive counter-attack. This is the version we recommend:

Over One Club and One Diamond, *Two Clubs* and *Two Diamonds* promise at least nine cards in the major suits. The normal range is about 6 to 11.

Over One Heart, *Two Hearts* is a sub-standard take-out double, always including five spades. This would be a typical hand at love all:

♠ Q 9 7 5 2   ♡ 6   ◊ A J 8 3   ♣ K 7 2

Over One Spade, *Two Spades* promises five hearts and a five-card minor, a hand such as:

♠ 6 3   ♡ K 10 8 6 4   ◊ 5   ♣ A K J 6 3

Over this bid of Two Spades, partner can inquire for the minor suit by bidding 2NT.

A player is not debarred from using these cue-bids on stronger hands that contain the right distribution. The bids can also be useful in competition:

South	West	North	East
1 ♠	No	1NT	2 ♠

East holds:

♠ 5 2   ♡ K J 9 7 4   ◊ A K 10 8 5 3   ♣ —

6. Defence to 1NT

In pairs play, especially, when so many opponents use a weak notrump throughout, it is essential to have conventional means of rocking the boat. Of the numerous conventions in existence, the Cansino defence is the most flexible. It works like this:

Against a *weak* notrump, bids in second or fourth position have this meaning:

Two Clubs signifies a hand playable in clubs and two other suits.

Two Diamonds signifies length in both majors.

Two Hearts and *Two Spades* are natural.

Double is primarily for penalties.

A variation occurs when the opponents are using a *strong* notrump or when the defender is a *passed* hand. In these circumstances a penalty double must of necessity be a dubious action. A *double* therefore indicates a touching two-suiter, and *Two Diamonds* signifies a hand playable in spades, hearts or diamonds. Other bids have the same meaning as above.

The virtue of the Cansino method lies in the frequency with

which it can be employed. Conventions such as Aspro or Landy, which are tied to particular suits, work well when the right hand comes along but too often the defender must remain mute.

7. Competitive doubles

There is not much profit to be gained from doubling low contracts when the opponents have found a fit. It is therefore sensible to find a different meaning for a double in an auction of this kind:

South	West	North	East
1 ◇	1 ♡	1 ♠	2 ♡
Dble			

The message of the double is: 'I have a useful hand but can think of no constructive bid that would express it well.' South might hold:

♠ A x   ♡ x x x   ◇ A Q x x x   ♣ K Q x

This is the general definition of a competitive double:

When opponents appear to have found a fit at a low level, a double is not for penalties but indicates general values.

Here the double is used by the defending side:

South	West	North	East
1 ♠	2 ♡	2 ♠	Dble

East is saying: 'I think it is our hand, but I am not sure in what denomination.' He might hold:

♠ 5 3   ♡ 6 4   ◇ A Q 7 6 2   ♣ K 10 8 4

A double of a forcing bid may be competitive even though opponents have not so far supported one another. The bidding goes:

South	West	North	East
1 ◇	1 ♡	2 ♣	Dble

East would not double Two Clubs for penalties in this sequence – at least, it would be foolish to do so. The double says: 'We probably have the balance of the cards, but neither Two Spades nor Two Hearts would be a good expression of my values.'

The opening side may make a competitive double at the Three level when each side has bid only one suit and when there is no space for any other form of game try.

South	West	North	East
1 ♡	2 ◇	2 ♡	3 ◇
Dble			

In this sequence Three Hearts by South on the second round would be competitive and not a game try. He has no room to bid a second suit without going beyond Three Hearts, so he makes a competitive double as a form of trial bid, inviting game in hearts.

8. Unassuming cue-bids

The phrase 'unassuming cue-bids' was first used in *Bridge for Tournament Players*, to describe an extension in the use of cue-bids in an opponent's suit. During part-score competition a cue-bid by a defender whose partner has made a simple overcall denotes at first a sound, as opposed to a competitive, raise. The bidding goes:

South	West	North	East
1 ♡	1 ♠	2 ♣	2 ♡

The first meaning of Two Hearts is: 'I can support your spades at least to the Two level, and my values are not simply distributional.' East might hold:

♠ J 7 4   ♡ 8 3   ◇ A 8 5 2   ♣ K 6 4 2

It follows – and this is perhaps the most valuable part of the convention – that when the defender's partner gives a direct raise, especially a jump raise, he is bidding defensively.

South	West	North	East
1 ♡	1 ♠	2 ♣	3 ♠

If East had a sound raise to Three Spades, with possibilities of game, he would first bid Two Hearts and later raise to Three Spades. As the bidding has gone, he will hold something of this nature:

♠ Q 10 7 4   ♡ 5   ◇ K J 7 4 3   ♣ 6 5 2

The point of the distinction between direct raise and unassuming cue-bid is to assist partner to judge how high to go in competition.

9. Negative doubles

The term 'sputnik double' is still common in Britain but has dropped out of fashion in America, where this type of double originated. The convention occurs when an overcall by second hand is doubled. Such a double proclaims, initially, a hand of about 7 to 10 points which presents no good natural call. South opens One Diamond, West overcalls with One Spade, and North holds:

♠ 6 5   ♡ K 8 6 4   ◇ Q 5 3   ♣ A 10 8 2

North has no suitable bid, but if he passes there is a danger that he may be shut out of the auction.

It will be noted that in the example above North holds four cards in the 'other major'. There are different ways of playing negative doubles, but we think the best results are obtained by following the style suggested by Jeremy Flint in his ferocious *Tiger Bridge*. In principle, a negative double of One Heart or One Spade promises four cards in the other major. A double of One Diamond (after One Club – One Diamond) promises support for both majors, and a double of One Spade after One Heart – One Spade promises support for both minors.

When the double is at the Two level the requirements are not so precise.

South	*West*	*North*	*East*
1 ♠	2 ♣	Dble	

The North hand should at least be playable in hearts. It would be right for South, on the next round, to introduce a poor suit of hearts rather than rebid a moderate suit of spades.

Players unused to negative doubles always raise the cry, 'But what happens when I want to double for penalties?' As a rule, you pass. If the next player passes, opener is *expected* to reopen, usually with a double, unless he has a minimum hand with such length in the enemy suit that it seems unlikely that his partner could be lying in wait.

It is usual to play negative doubles up to the level of Three Hearts. They are often very welcome when an opponent has made a pre-emptive overcall.

Many players use negative doubles only on the sort of moderate hands we have described. Some advantage can be derived, however, from doubling on quite good hands as well. For one thing, the double is economical and you get a picture of partner's hand from the way in which he responds to it.

As we have noted, a player who doubles on a moderate 7 to 10 is expected (1) to have certain distributional features and (2) not to speak again unless prodded by partner. When a player does speak again without encouragement, he shows the values for a response at the level of Two and cancels the information previously given about his distribution. The bidding begins:

South	West	North	East
1 ♡	2 ♣	?	

North holds:

(1)   ♠ 8 5   ♡ 10 2   ◇ A K 9 7 4   ♣ Q 8 5 2

North bids Two Diamonds, forcing for one round, just as he would have done if West had passed.

(2)   ♠ A Q 10 6 3   ♡ 7 6   ◇ A 9 4   ♣ J 5 3

The best way to progress is by a negative double. (Two Spades, as we shall see in a moment, would not be forcing.) Say that South rebids Two Hearts. North then bids Two Spades, forcing.

(3)   ♠ K J 9 7 5 2   ♡ 6   ◇ Q 8 5 2   ♣ 10 4

Now North bids Two Spades, non-forcing, which is just what he would like to do. You see the distinction? In (1) North was responding in a lower-valued suit and his bid has the normal sense; here he is responding in a higher suit than partner's.

Similarly, a bid at the Three level is limited and non-forcing.

South	West	North	West
1 ♠	2 ♡	3 ♣	

With a fairly good hand, North would double. His bid of Three Clubs is non-forcing – an arrangement that may suit him very well.

Terence Reese and Albert Dormer
How to Play a Good Game of Bridge 60p

'This is the book for anyone who wants to make the transition from a pusher of paste-board to a capable and intelligent player'
SUNDAY TIMES

'Of high quality . . . particularly recommended for rubber bridge players. It simplifies the technical intricacies of both bidding and play and should convert losing players into winners'
SUNDAY TELEGRAPH

Basil Dalton
The Complete Patience Book 75p

You may be alone . . . but you'll never be lonely when you discover the pleasure of patience. You'll find hours of absorbing but relaxing activity in this complete guide to a fascinating pastime . . . An authority on card games, the late Basil Dalton was an expert on patience. Here, in one volume, are the results of his years of interest in the subject. Some are easy, some are more difficult – all provide a unique form of mental exercise and entertainment.

Oswald Jacoby and John R. Crawford
The Backgammon Book £1.50

A complete, up-to-date, step-by-step guide on how to play backgammon for love or money – and win. Written by two world champions and illustrated with large, precise diagrams, this essential guide ranges from the crucial opening moves to the finer points of the middle and end games.

In addition to probability tables, etiquette and the official rules of the International Backgammon Association, there are chapters on the history of the game, how to run a tournament and how to play chouette (backgammon for more than two people) plus a useful glossary.

Rixi Markus
Common-sense Bridge 50p

Although good technique is essential for a player of championship class, something much more personal is also needed — a bridge philosophy.

Internationally acknowledged as one of the world's greatest players, Rixi Markus expounds on her own ideas and those adopted from great masters. Using illustrative hands to take the reader through every aspect of bidding and play, she shares her remarkable insights to produce a sure signpost to better and more enjoyable bridge.

Hubert Phillips
Pan Book of Card Games £1.25.

No other book of card games explains so many games — 50 card games and 28 games of patience — so thoroughly or offcrs so much instruction. With its lucid descriptions and its innumerable specimen hands played out card by card, it will afford hours of entertainment.

'Amarillo Slim' Preston
Play Poker to Win 60p

Reading Slim's book is like looking over his shoulder at the card table for a personal lesson in winning. He explains in detail the strategy and tactics of poker, how to bet, how to gauge the opposition's strong and weak points, when to bluff, when to drop and when to pick up your chips and head for home. His narrative is unassuming, quick-paced and spiced with colourful anecdotes of big-time gambling.

Gavin and Bernard Lyall
Operation Warboard £1

How to fight World War II battles in miniature!

'Famous thriller writer Gavin Lyall and his son Bernard combine forces to produce a very different wargames book which focuses on battles of World War II in 20/25mm scale . . . extremely readable' MILITARY MODELLING

'How a modern wargame is played; where and how you can purchase, convert or scratch-build your models; how to design and build suitable battlegrounds' BATTLE MAGAZINE

Margaret Allen
The Money Book £1.75

Work out your income properly, fill in your tax return; make the best use of your bank; buy a freezer, a house or a car; decide on an allowance for your children; understand a company annual report; make a will; get a divorce; invest in unit trusts or buy by mail order . . .

'The most comprehensive book about money' MANCHESTER EVENING NEWS

Brian Moynahan
Airport International £1.25

The sensational book that takes the lid off the world of international air travel. How smugglers operate, and how they're caught . . . when and how luggage is pilfered . . . how air traffic control really works . . . how airports cope with a crash landing . . . which are the dangerous airports that pilots try to avoid . . . your chances of survival in an air crash.

Based on extensive research by Brian Moynahan of the *Sunday Times Insight* team.

Ronald Lewin
Slim: The Standardbearer £1.50

The life of Field-Marshal the Viscount Slim of Yarralumla and
Bishopston, commander of the 14th Army and hero of the Burma
campaign, Governor-General of Australia.

'Not only military history at its best, but biography at its best'
THE LISTENER

'The name of Bill Slim represents so perfectly all that the
British Army has ever looked for in its Captains . . . this fine
biography makes one appreciate his true greatness not merely
as an almost unique Soldier and Commander, but also as a man'
BRITISH ARMY REVIEW

Patrick Meehan
Innocent Villain 80p

He was raised on streets of one of Europe's most violent slums.
In Borstal at eighteen — serving his apprenticeship in crime.
Acknowledged in the criminal world of Glasgow as a 'peterman' — a
master safe-cracker. Sentenced to life for robbery and murder — then
pardoned by Royal decree. In this book, Patrick Meehan
tells how and why he was framed. Framed by British Intelligence.
Astonishing allegations that demand an answer from the highest
in the land.

You can buy these and other Pan books from booksellers and
newsagents; or direct from the following address:
Pan Books, Sales Office, Cavaye Place, London SW10 9PG
Send purchase price plus 20p for the first book and 10p for
each additional book, to allow for postage and packing
Prices quoted are applicable in the UK

While every effort is made to keep prices low, it is sometimes
necessary to increase prices at short notice. Pan Books reserve
the right to show on covers and charge new retail prices which
may differ from those advertised in the text or elsewhere